C000161351

TOUBAB

AN AFRICAN ADVENTURE

ROB COUGHLIN

For my Dad without whose help none of this would have happened.

For Adama who caught me when I was falling.

For my amazing son Joe who is my shining light.

For the people of The Gambia, for whom I hold a lasting love and affection.

And especially for my wonderful mum, Mildred, Ellen, McCluskey, who is an eternal source of inspiration and strength to me, as I finally begin to find my way through the trials and tribulations of life without the anaesthetic.

Introduction

In December 2001 my mum was diagnosed with a recurrence of the breast cancer that had afflicted her some 20 years previously, and this time the prognosis was terminal. I was 6 years sober, and I knew that to stay in England would mean almost certain relapse, so I decided to do something I had always wanted to do. I bought a second-hand Peugeot 405 diesel estate car, filled it full of gear from an army surplus shop, and three days before she died, set off in the general direction of North Africa. I drove through Spain, Morocco, The Western Sahara, Mauritania, across 500 miles of the Sahara Desert, and finally arrived in The Gambia, via Senegal. In The Gambia I met an African dancer called Adama, we got married, and a year later she gave birth to our son. I started a small fishing business on the beach and for the next three years lived pretty much as an African fisherman. This book describes the journey to The Gambia, and the adventures that Adama and I had while I was there.

During my time in The Gambia, I was involved in a full-scale riot at an African Nations football match, spent time on a desert island off the coast of Guinea Bissau, was involved in a dispute, with the neighbours, that was only resolved by the intervention of armed soldiers, and I saved a man from drowning in rough seas off the coast of the main tourist beach in The Gambia.

The book describes life in The Gambia from a more local perspective, and introduces the reader to the people, and landscape, of this tiny nation in West Africa.

© OpenStreetMap contributors

© OpenStreetMap contributors

Chapter 1 – The Catalyst

It was Christmas Day 2001, I was up at my parent's house in Nottingham, and we had just sat down to our Christmas dinner. As usual, my mum had pulled out all the stops. I looked down at my plate, and as well as the traditional turkey there were little sausages wrapped in bacon, beautifully cooked roast potatoes, carrots and parsnips cooked in butter, big balls of stuffing and of course Brussels sprouts. On the table were boats full of gravy and bread sauce.

My mum had come down to London to visit me in November, and I had been shocked at the time at how frail she had looked. As we began eating it soon became apparent to me that if anything she had got a little worse. She raised a forkful of potato to her lips and made a brave attempt to swallow it. She pecked away at her food like that for a few minutes before putting her knife and fork down, and conceding defeat. With tears in my eyes, I got up from the table, and went down to the bathroom. Once in there I cried my eyes out. I was 6 years sober at that time, and I couldn't bear the thought that I was going to lose my mum.

I knew that the breast cancer she had been diagnosed with 20 years earlier had returned, and I knew when she was unable to swallow her food that it was the beginning of the end. Nobody had actually told me that, but they didn't have to, I just knew with every fibre of my being that my mum had run out of luck. The hospital had stopped the Tamoxifen that had been working so well for her, for so many years, and now the cancer had re-asserted itself, and was raging through her body. My mum had always been a fighter, but this time she had finally been outgunned, and outmanoeuvred, by the rapacious illness that had made such an unwelcome return.

I had known my mum was very ill when she had come down to visit me, and I had suspected then that this Christmas would be her last with us, but knowing it didn't make it any easier for any of us to deal with. When I was a child, my mum and Dad had always left a Christmas stocking at the end of the bed for my brother and I, and this Christmas I returned the favour. I had been collecting little bits and pieces for them both since the previous summer, and on Christmas Eve, after they had gone to bed, I had left them each a bag of presents outside their bedroom door

It was a Christmas of very mixed emotions. I was happy to be with my family, but heartbroken, and terrified, by my mum's condition, and the prospect of losing her. Christmas passed in a bit of a blur, and I returned to my flat in King's Cross with a heavy heart. Slowly an idea began formulating in my head. I knew that when my mum died, I would lose my tenuous grip on sobriety, as I was still way too dependent on her, and in spite of my deep unhappiness at my mum's situation, my thoughts began to turn to Africa.

Since my early teens, I had been fascinated by Africa. I could recall blasting out "Rock the Casbah", by the Clash, in the late 70's, while vague ideas of Marrakesh, and The Paris-Dakar rally ran through my mind. Later on, at University, it had been Joseph Conrad's "Heart of Darkness", that had captured my imagination, suggesting dark forces at work, in a wild and primitive place. I had travelled through a large part of Africa before, in my late twenties, on an organised Overland adventure tour. I had stood on the edge of Victoria Falls, before Bungee-jumping off Victoria Fall's bridge. I had seen the vastness of the Ngorongoro crater, and stalked the rare white rhino on foot. I had seen a wide variety of animals in

4

their natural habitat, from the crocodiles that lurked at the edge of water pools, to the lions, zebras, and giraffes, that roamed the plains. I had almost walked headlong into a Green Mamba that had disguised itself as a branch of a tree, and I had very nearly been torn limb from limb by a troop of angry Baboons, that I had disturbed on a reckless cycle into the bush in Zimbabwe. I had stood on the top of Table Mountain, and marvelled at the views, but in reality, all I had done was scratch the surface of a place, and a way of life, that was totally alien to me.

I, after all, had grown up in a leafy London suburb, where the only dangerous wildlife was the gang of boys on the estate down the road who would occasionally try to steal my pushbike if I ventured to close to their patch. Across the road from my house was an old church, and behind that were some woods, and incredibly, an old Franciscan monastery. I spent many happy days building camps in the woods, and even before I was a teenager, I revelled in being out in the wild, even if the woods were only a stone's throw from the comfort, and security, of the family home.

I was always rather in awe of the mysterious figures that the monks cut, in what otherwise was just another ordinary part of greater London, and I was blessed that my parents had chosen so wisely where to buy their first home. In my early teens my parents took my brother, and I, on a succession of what were, at the time, quite exotic holidays. We visited Spain, Malta, the old Yugoslavia, Ibiza,(before it became the party island it now is), and had one memorable trip to the U.S.A to visit my auntie who lived in New York State.

I was flown over Niagara Falls in a helicopter, and taken right next to it on board "The Maid of the Mist". We went behind the falls in the caves, and the month that we spent in America was an amazing, and fantastic, experience for me. I had always thirsted for a life beyond the mental, and physical, restrictions of my immediate environment, and these early holidays showed me that there was a life beyond homework, and my daily tube train journeys to school, which because of my extreme self-consciousness, I found to be a bit of an ordeal. From a very early age I had felt suffocated by convention, and Africa seemed to offer the freedom, and adventure, that I so badly craved.

When I left school, I worked in the construction industry, as a trainee site agent, labouring by day, and going to college in the evenings. When I was made redundant after a couple of years, I worked as a despatch rider, until I punctured my lung in a bad crash, and then I half-heartedly tried to make a career for myself as a Tax Collector, and a Betting shop manager. After a couple of years of doing nothing in particular, I took myself off to university, when I was 28 years old, to study English Literature, and Writing and Publishing. I excelled at my studies, and even though I was drinking a bottle of whiskey every other day, I still managed to be named as the player of the year for the University 2nd eleven football team.

I was halfway through my second year at Middlesex University when I was run over by a 17-ton lorry while cycling to Kings Cross station one morning. I sustained some horrific injuries, and when I finally came out of the hospital, after spending 3 weeks in intensive care, and another two months in agonising pain, and extreme discomfort, on a general ward, I was evicted from where I was living, and my girlfriend at the time found it all too much to deal with, and walked out on me. Left alone in a small council flat that my girlfriend had managed to arrange before she went, and still with some horrendous injuries that required daily visits from the district nurse, I descended into alcoholism, and emerged battered, and bruised, from the psychiatric system when I was in my early thirties. I discovered a set of support groups, and spent the next six years attending meetings, and apart from occasional self-medicating with powerful antipsychotic medication, enjoyed a period of relative stability, and calm. That stability and calm had evaporated now that the cancer had finally begun to overwhelm my mum, and I knew that there was only one way that I could try and deal with it. I had to go to Africa.

All throughout the misery of my twenties, and early thirties, my mum had been a rock. She had stood by me through the dark depressions that characterised my advancing alcoholism, and was always on the end of the phone, or prepared to send me that extra money when needed, for an outstanding electric bill, or some crisis or other. We had built up a very close friendship in the time that I had been sober, but because of my over-dependence on her, I couldn't imagine how I would cope if she wasn't around.

When my mum was ill she would regularly phone me up, and say that she wanted to see me. Each time I went to visit her, she would give me her cash card, and tell me to take out a few hundred pounds. I started going on mad road trips on my motorbike. One day I just took off and went to the Isle of Wight, sleeping under Shanklin pier, rather than paying for a bed and breakfast. Another time I packed the tent, and roared off to Cornwall, taking in the majesty of Stonehenge on the way. Next, I bought a plane ticket to Malaga, where I took the train to Algecieras, with a view to going to Morocco. On the ferry to Tangiers, I got chatting to a Mexican journalist called Hortensia, who was travelling to Morocco with her girlfriend. They had a row during the journey, and the girlfriend headed back to Spain.

Hortensia was very short, slightly dumpy, and had short frizzy hair. She was also a lesbian, and I wasn't particularly attracted to her, but we made some kind of a connection, and we decided to hook up together. My new travelling companion and I hired a car, and set off to drive around Morocco. We headed South East to Fes, and then to Erfoud, on the edge of the Sahara Desert. The night-time drives through the Atlas Mountains were both terrifying, and exhilarating, in equal measure. Hortensia turned out to be just as reckless a driver as myself, and it was only by good fortune that our trip wasn't brought to a sudden and bloody end, as a result of one of our suicidal overtaking manoeuvres, on one of the many blind bends that typified the various mountain passes that we drove through.

We spent a night in the desert near Erfoud, and then headed west, until we arrived at the Dades Gorge, and camped up for the night at the foot of its towering face. We had picked up a couple of Spanish hitchhikers, and we set up our tents next to each other. The Spaniards were both blokes in their early twenties, and they invited Hortensia and I into their tent to smoke some hashish, and listen to some music. As I was in recovery I declined, and as I sat in the tent on my own, listening to the music and laughter coming out of theirs, I found myself becoming more and more jealous of the fun they seemed to be having. After a while, I couldn't stand it any longer, and I burst out of my tent in what can only be described as a fit of jealous pique. I had no desire to join them, but what could I do? I saw the steep slope of the ravine in front of me, and I decided to climb to the top.

It took me almost two hours to get to the top of the gorge, and when I did I heard a noise that made my blood freeze. Against the backdrop of a luminescent full moon, came what I thought was the unmistakable sound of a pack of howling wolves. Suddenly I became acutely aware of how vulnerable I was up there, at the top of the gorge, on my own, in the middle of the night. My travelling companions were a long way away, and would be of absolutely no help to me if anything happened, so I began hastily scrambling my way back down the slope towards the tents.

I reached the bottom in a quarter of the time it had taken to reach the top, and as I was making my way back to the tent, I spotted the skull of a dead sheep. I thought it would be fun to tease my travelling companions, so before I climbed inside my tent I left it sitting on the bonnet of the car, knowing that they would discover it in the morning. Hortensia came back to the tent about half an hour after me, and I said nothing to her about what I had been doing while she had been away. I was still feeling a bit jealous, so I wished her goodnight, turned over, and went to sleep.

In the morning it soon became apparent that my little stunt with the sheep's head was paying dividends. I awoke to a lot of excited chatter outside, and when I poked my head out of the tent flap, I saw our two Spanish friends standing by the car bonnet, and eyeing the sheep's skull nervously." Who do you think left it there?" said the elder of the two to me. I feigned surprise, and suggested that maybe it was some kind of warning. "Perhaps somebody doesn't want us here", I said, "maybe we should just pack up and get out of here". Everyone agreed, so we hurriedly packed everything, jumped into the car, and got ready to leave. The looks on their faces were priceless, and I just couldn't contain myself any longer. I burst out laughing, and pointed at the sheep's head that was now lying on the ground next to the car. "Maybe it was trying to tell you to keep the music down last night," I said. "It was you, wasn't it?" said one of the Spaniards, "filo de puta," said the other. I couldn't bring myself to tell them how jealous I had been feeling the previous night, so I tried to just laugh it off. It didn't wash with Hortensia though, and I could tell that she was deeply disappointed with me for acting so childishly.

The next part of our journey saw us continuing west, skirting the edge of the Anti-Atlas mountains, and heading towards the Atlantic coast. We dropped the Spaniards off in a little town, along the way, and we were hurtling along the road when a Moroccan policeman seemed to materialise out of nowhere, and was standing in front of us, in the middle of the road. He quickly flagged us down, and ordered us to stop. I pulled over to the side of the road, got out of the Peugeot, and left Hortensia sitting nervously in the passenger seat.

The policeman was impeccably dressed, and his clothes were crisp, and spotless. He had a very friendly demeanour, and a distinctly ethereal air about him. "You should not drive so fast", he said, "this road is very dangerous, many people are killed here". He asked for my documents, as I was driving at the time, and when he saw that they were in order he sent us on our way with a friendly wave, and a further caution against driving too fast.

Both Hortensia and I had felt the same about the policeman. Neither of us could work out where he had appeared from in an otherwise deserted road, with no other vehicle such as a police car in sight. He made a deep impression on both of us, and I decided to drop my speed a bit. It was just as well I did, for on the next blind bend I momentarily lost control of the car, and veered across the centreline into the path of an oncoming lorry. At the last second I yanked the wheel to the right, and half closed my eyes, as a collision seemed inevitable. The left side of the car briefly scraped against the truck with a horrible screeching sound, and then we were clear.

When I pulled up to check for damage on our hire car, the significance of our encounter with the policeman hit me hard. Before I had left for this trip I had been reading something called "The Angel Script." "The Angel Script" proposed the idea that everywhere in life there are angels in human form that exist to guide and protect us. This notion had really appealed to me, and it seemed to me at the time that our friendly policeman had been one of these angels, put in our way to protect, and save us. I told Hortensia what I was thinking, and far from laughing at me, she embraced the idea, and told me that she agreed with me. Between us we decided that our policeman friend had been one of these supernatural beings, and with this in mind, I took it easy for the rest of the day. It could, of course, just been one of those everyday events that we had attached our own significance to, but to this day, even with the benefit of hindsight, I'm still more inclined to believe the angel theory.

We carried on west, driving past the blossoming almond trees on the edge of the Anti- Atlas Mountains, and finally pitched up the tent on a campsite near Agadir. We stayed on the beach for a few days, soaking up the hot African sun, and swimming in the warm Atlantic Ocean, and then we drove north to return the car in Tangiers. I had learned a few tricks from my travelling companion along the way. Hortensia was forever producing her press credentials to get freebies, and special treatment, and when we got to the ferry she told the man in charge that she was doing a special story on the port, and as such she shouldn't have to pay the full fare for the ferry crossing. He was pleased to be the subject of interest, and after taking a few pictures of him, and assuring him that he would be featured in the article, we got a substantial discount on the fare. I felt slightly uncomfortable at Hortensia's deceit, but as I was by now extremely low on cash, I went along willingly with her charade.

We returned to London, and Hortensia moved in with me in my little flat in King's Cross. It didn't last long though, as I soon realised that her habit of getting everything for free extended to me as well, and I quickly became tired of it, and asked her to leave.

By now I had formulated a plan. My mum was gradually getting weaker, and weaker, and I knew that once she had died there would be nothing to keep me rooted in the UK, so the question seemed to be how could I organise it so I could leave for an indeterminate amount of time, while I came to terms with her death?

I decided to decorate my flat, and rent it out while I was away. I bought a ten-year-old Peugeot 405 diesel estate car to take the place of my ZXR400 motorbike that had spontaneously burst into flames when I was visiting a friend in London, and while visiting my Mum in Nottingham I went to an army surplus shop, and stocked up on survival, and camping gear.

I bought a pair of eight-foot steel sand ladders that fitted neatly in the back of the Peugeot, and I bought some jerry cans for water, and diesel. I assembled a medical kit to take with me, that included a D.I.Y malaria injection in case I was afflicted in an area where there was no immediate help, and an assortment of bandages, and potions. I obtained a Mauritanian Visa from the embassy in Berkeley square, and I got the phone number of the receptionist while I was at it. I tiled my bathroom floor, and advertised for a tenant. I had a selection of jabs at the British Airways office in Regent Street, and bought a number of roadmaps of Morocco, and West Africa.

Next I took the car on a series of road trips, to familiarise myself with any problems it might develop on the journey, and I fixed a few niggling things that showed up along the way. I drove down to Cornwall for a few days, sleeping in the car wherever I ended up, and I took a trip to Fort William in Scotland, where I hiked to the top of Ben Nevis while I was there. By the end of November 2002 I was ready to go, so I rented my flat out, and left, not knowing when, or if ever, I would return.

All that was left now were the goodbyes. First I headed to Nottingham to see my mum one last time. There really was nothing left of her now. The cancer had quite literally eaten her away, and it was heart-breaking to see how ill she had become. Her skin was paper thin, and I doubt if she weighed more than 6 stone. Her spirit though was as indomitable as ever, and even at this late stage of her illness she was still refusing painkilling medication, as she wanted to keep a clear head for as long as she possibly could. I think it must have been obvious even to her that the game was up though, and I wanted to keep things as light-hearted as possible when I saw her.

By now she was too ill to do much talking, so I sat by her bed, and held her hand. As I got up to leave the last words she said to me were, "see you soon love". It was typical of my Mum that even though she knew she was dying, she still wanted to reassure me that things were going to be ok. I left my Dad sitting stoically by her bedside, and I walked out of the hospital for the last time. My dad is a very tough, and loyal, man, and I knew that there was nothing I could do, or say, that would make what was happening to my mum any easier to bear for him. As much as it pained me, I had to leave him to his grief, and not let my own grief overwhelm me.

I headed straight from the hospital to a friend's house in London. This was my oldest friend Mason, who was more like a big brother to me than anything. He had long since given up trying to dissuade me from leaving, and he tried his best to be supportive of what I was doing. We went to see his grandfather Harry, and he gave me

13

an old army bayonet to take with me that he had kept since World War Two.

After saying goodbye to Mason, and his family, I headed to Worthing to see my real older brother Joe, and his family. He and his wife were also very welcoming, and after two days playing with my young nieces, I got some last minute tools for the journey, and set off for Portsmouth to catch the ferry.

Chapter 2 – On the Road

My Dad had paid for the ferry crossing from Portsmouth to Bilbao, and as I relaxed in the cabin, I thought about the journey ahead. I almost couldn't contain the excitement that was bubbling up inside me. I was finally doing it, I was going to Africa, and I was doing it on my own terms. I wasn't part of a cosseted group of tourists, shielded from the harsh realities of life of the places I would be visiting; I was as self-reliant as I could possibly be. I was living my childhood dream, and in spite of what had happened to my Mum, I was happy.

The boat journey passed quickly, and as I drove off the ferry in Bilbao, the sun was shining, and my heart was singing. I drove through Spain in a day, passing close by the mountains in the centre of the country, and I drove through the middle of the medieval city of Seville. Apart from the necessity of getting fuel from time to time, it never occurred to me to stop in Spain. My mind was set on Africa, and I was on a mission.

I rolled into Algeciras after 17 hours of more or less continuous driving, and I parked up by the ferry terminal. The next boat wasn't due until the morning, so I had a whole night to kill. I popped out to get some sandwiches, and immediately sensed that this was no place to be careless. Algeciras is a border town, and my previous experience of border towns was that they were dangerous places, best avoided if you could, and if that wasn't possible, stayed in for as short a time as was necessary. I decided to sleep in the car, and stretched out in the passenger seat, with a piece of lead piping in the door-well, close to hand. I was awoken in the middle of the night by the sound of the car's horn, and someone rapping on my windscreen. In my sleep my foot had ended up resting on the horn, so I changed my position, and went back to my dreams.

The ferry was due to leave at 6am, so I got up early, and headed down to the port. I drove down the slipway, and stopped at the checkpoint. There were no European niceties here. My passport was inspected, I paid the fare, and then drove on to the slightly dilapidated boat. The ferry crossing would only take a couple of hours, so I found a space on deck, and stretched out in the sun. I could feel Africa approaching, and I luxuriated in the knowledge that I would soon be on African soil again. The sun seemed to have a special kind of warmth to it, and I observed my travelling companions, who were chattering excitedly in a baffling variety of languages. I thought I could pick up Spanish, French, possibly some Eastern European, and a wide variety of African dialects, and the chattering was music to my ears.

All too soon we arrived at Tangiers, and I drove off the ferry into Moroccan customs. My passport, and the documentation of the car were checked again, and the customs officer looked at me expectantly. I tossed him a couple of packs of cigarettes, and a large Toblerone. This seemed to satisfy him, and he waved me on with a smile. I learned from this that a smile, and a little bit of generosity, could take you a long way on this continent. It was beginning to dawn on me that there was nothing more disagreeable to a poor person, than a comparatively rich person, who appeared to be both miserable, and arrogant.

I smiled, and waved, my way through the rest of customs, and then headed straight for the road to Casablanca. Bowling along the surprisingly good road I burst into song. My troubles were behind me, and I had an almost supernatural feeling of being safe, and looked after. My Guardian Angel, I felt, was alive and well, and watching over my every move.

This happy state persisted for several hours, until I reached the outskirts of the city. I took the road around the city centre, and as I was driving under a bridge, I noticed some movement on top of it, out of the corner of my eye. The next second I swerved drastically to avoid a slab of concrete that had been hurled off the top of the bridge by two youths, and was heading straight for my windscreen. I just missed it, and as I drove on I alternately cursed the two youths, and thanked my Guardian Angel for keeping me safe. It was a close call but I was ready for anything on this trip, and this near miss just reminded me to stay vigilant, and keep on my guard.

I continued south for several more hours, until I reached the campsite I had stayed in during my trip around Morocco with Hortensia, some months previously. This was located about five miles outside Agadir, and was full of expensive looking German camper vans, with satellite dishes on their roofs. Feeling like the poor relation in my little Peugeot, I pulled in, and set up my tent directly on the beach. I had been driving continuously for 16 hours, and it was such a relief to stop at last. The Peugeot had, quite staggeringly, been giving me almost 70 miles to the gallon, and was proving itself the ideal choice for my journey. The £500 that it had cost me definitely seemed to have been money well spent, and it was becoming apparent that I had got a real bargain.

By now I was enjoying lovely hot sunny days, and I decided to stay on this campsite for the best part of a week. Mornings would find me trotting up into the hills that lay behind the beach, to do my ablutions, before coming back down to the tent, and boiling up some instant noodles for breakfast from my store of dried foodstuffs. The rest of the day would be spent diving in and out of the beautiful Atlantic Ocean that washed up to the edge of my tent, and lying on the sand, soaking up the warm Moroccan sun.

At night I would read a few pages of "Jupiter's Travels", by Ted Simon, by torchlight, and then I'd finish off with a late night smoke, and reflect on the miles travelled, and the miles still to go.

One day I decided to walk along the shoreline to Agadir. I had been walking for about three miles when I came across a wall stretching across the sand, and running down to the sea. I had to walk up and around it, and it seemed to border some kind of official, and heavily guarded, building. Knowing how easy it was to be taken for a spy in certain countries, I resisted the urge to photograph it, and kept on walking with my camera safely hidden away in my pocket.

In Agadir I was struck by the beauty of some of the women. When I was in the local supermarket, one, in particular, caught my eye. She had long black hair, and the most amazing green eyes, and it was only the thought of appearing foolish that prevented me from approaching her and declaring my undying love on the spot.

After mooching around Agadir for a couple of hours, I decided to go to an internet café to get some news from home. There was an e-mail from my Dad, it read, "Mum died 6th Dec", three days after I had left the UK. My Dad later told me that very soon after I had left, my Mum finally began taking the morphine she was prescribed to alleviate her pain, and she soon slipped away from us.

I had a very strange sensation on the bus back to the campsite. There were some children playing together a couple of seats in front of me, and I felt a sudden surge of love and affection for them. My Mum had always loved children, and I couldn't help feeling that for a brief second her spirit had touched me deep in my soul.

I had been on the campsite for nearly a week, enjoying the time, and getting used to the hot African sun, and the strong Atlantic breakers, but the news about my mum jolted me back into reality. I packed up my little tent, and the rest of my bits and pieces, and headed south into The Western Sahara, stopping on the way to fill my Jerry cans with plenty of diesel, and water.

After about 50 miles or so, I saw a figure at the side of the road. It was a Berber tribesman, easily identified by the bright green headscarf he wore. All the different Arab tribesmen wear particular colours. The Berbers wear green, the Tuaregs of Tunisia wear blue, and the Bedouin tribes of The Sinai wear a red and white chequered headdress. I pulled over, let him in, and after employing a bit of sign language to work out where he was headed, I took a detour up into the surrounding hills to drop him off. We passed blazing white villages on the sides of the hills, painted to reflect the Sun's fierce rays, and I let him out of the car, in what appeared to be the middle of nowhere. I retraced my route back to the main road, and headed back towards Tarfaya, which was the next town on the way to the Sahara desert.

An hour or so later I saw a girl standing on the side of the road. She was white, European, and seemed to be on her own. I thought my luck was in, and pulled up to give her a lift, when a guy in his mid-twenties popped up out of the undergrowth. I had been caught by the oldest trick in the book. Nice looking girl shows a bit of leg, and a gullible car driver, in this instance me, pulls over and gets to meet her boyfriend too.

They turned out to be a young Swiss couple called Maurice, and Anna, and they were on their way to Casamance, in Southern Senegal, where they hoped to stay in a house owned by one of their friends. Maurice was a white Rastafarian, and apparently there was a big Rastafarian community where they were headed.

They were carrying huge rucksacks, and somehow I managed to squeeze them, and their luggage, into the trusty Peugeot, and we all carried on south together.

As it transpired this part of the journey wasn't to be without incident. I was bombing along at a steady 60 miles an hour, when I suddenly lost the road, and hurtled toward what appeared to be a grainy wall in front of me. I braced myself for impact, shouted a warning to Maurice and Anna, and slammed on the brakes. The car came to a juddering halt, buried up to the grill in a massive pile of sand, and I turned round to check on my passengers. Maurice and Anna were both okay so we dug the car out, and assessed the situation.

An enormous sand drift had blown across the road, but there seemed to be a way around it. The car had somehow not been damaged, and it wasn't far to Tarfaya, so we carried on, albeit rather more cautiously than before. We arrived in Tarfaya just before dark, and found a place to stay in a cheap guest house. The accommodation was very basic, and I had the same feeling in Tarfaya that I had had in Algeciras. In short it looked, and felt, like a den of thieves.

Tarfaya was like a town you would see in a Wild West movie. Sand and dust blown streets stretched out in all directions, poker-faced people went about their daily business, and the mangiest curs you are ever likely to see, seemed to be fighting over scraps on every street corner. It was no surprise when I reflected that Tarfaya was pretty much a border town too, thus giving weight to my theory about said towns.

The theory received the ultimate endorsement when I set about moving some bits and pieces into my hotel room. Two guys along the corridor beckoned me over to show me something in their room. I rather naively went over to them, and almost before I knew what was happening, they grabbed me and tried to pull me in. I saw a flash of silver in one of their hands, which was almost certainly a knife, and decided that there was no way that I was going in the room with them. I head-butted one of them, and my knee found the groin of the other. They reeled back and let go, and I ran back to my room, and locked the door.

All I could think about now were the potential consequences of this exchange. Would they go and get their friends? Would they cause trouble for me with the hotel? Would they get the police involved? This last thought bothered me a great deal. As an unbeliever in a radical Muslim area, I doubted whether the police would be too sympathetic towards me, and I figured that they would be more likely to throw me in jail than listen to my side of the story. I sat in my room for a couple of hours digesting these unpleasant thoughts, and when I felt the coast was clear I sneaked out, and told Maurice and Anna what had happened. They advised me to keep a low profile, brought me some dinner to my room, and after a few anxious hours the rest of the evening passed without incident.

The next day I was walking down what passed for the high street, when a very ragged man began haranguing me as I walked past. A passerby who spoke English told me that the man had a grievance towards Westerners, and particularly their Governments, and it appeared that I presented a convenient target for him. After what had happened the previous night I was in no mood for this, and I began having a stand-up row with him in the middle of the street, much to the amusement of the local population, who looked slightly bemused to see a Westerner behaving in such an uncool manner. I finally walked away to the safety of some buildings and pondered my reaction. I came to the conclusion that it was pure arrogance on my part, and fear and resentment on his. I represented all that he had come to despise, and fear, in the small World that he inhabited, and I had acted true to how he would have expected me to act, uncaring, and full of my own importance. He had acted true to type as well, and the result had been an unpleasant clash of cultures and ideals.

Maurice, Anna, and I, went out for a coffee later that evening, and sitting opposite us was the man I had been arguing with, and three of his friends. I sent a round of teas over to them, and walked over, apologised, and offered out my hand. He took it, and as we sat back down at our respective tables an air of mutual respect settled over all concerned. We parted as friends, and I realised that I still had a lot to learn about the effect I was having on the people around me, as I swept through their individual Worlds with my comparative wealth, and Western ideals. I was to learn a lot more about myself, and the people of West Africa before this adventure had run its course.

Chapter 3 – Desert Trials

After leaving Tarfaya we headed to a town called Dahkla, and I took the opportunity to get a last minute modification done to the car while we were there. I got a local mechanic to weld a plate over the engine sump as protection against the rocks we would be bound to encounter in the desert, and I checked the oil and water levels, as I had done every day since I had left the UK. The daytime temperatures were rising rapidly the further South I got, and the coolant in the radiator would soon evaporate if I didn't keep my eye on it, so I made sure that checking the levels was part of my daily routine.

On one of the days I spent in Dahkla I took my bicycle out of the car, and went for a look at the local area. I discovered a huge outdoor market on the outskirts of town, and as I cycled around, I had the strong feeling that I was an unwelcome intrusion on the lives of the everyday people I came into contact with. I was getting some quite unfriendly looks, so I scooted around for a bit, and then headed back to my room in the cheap guesthouse that the three of us were staying in.

The next day I set off for Nouhadibou in Mauritania, with Maurice and Anna still in tow. The road was still good, and all was going well, when we approached a random army checkpoint that had been set up in the middle of the road. I pulled over, and the three of us got out of the car. There were four or five soldiers standing around looking bored, with their rifles slung conspicuously over their shoulders. They asked for our passports, so we handed them over, and I went to sit down on what appeared to be some kind of blanket in the sand that I had noticed while the soldiers were talking to us.

Immediately one of them shouted out to me, ran over, and hauled me roughly to my feet. It seemed that I had unwittingly sat down on the mat they all used for their daily prayers, and they were shocked, and angry, at my unintentional show of disrespect. The soldier who had dragged me to my feet pointed his rifle at me, and asked if I was crazy or sick. I was feeling a little light-headed, so I pointed to my head, and screwed my eyes up as if I were in pain, and after a lot of grovelling his attitude softened a little, and then, when a small bribe was paid, we were back on our way.

We arrived at the campsite just before dark, and began to put our tents up. At the campsite were a number of fellow over-landers in a varied assortment of vehicles. There was a group of German lads in a Mercedes, and a 4 wheel drive, there were a Swiss couple in an old camper van, there were a couple of other cars, and there was even one hardy fellow on a motorbike. Maurice and Anna were still with me, so we joined up with the other vehicles, and started to look for a guide to take us across the desert. In a very short space of time we had enlisted the services of a local Mauritanian Arab called Mohammed.

Mohammed was in his early fifties, wore a blue turban, and had a slightly wizened sunburnt face. He was very insistent that he could carry us safely across the desert, so we pooled our money together, and gave him $150 for his services.

After buying my compulsory Mauritanian car insurance, I decided to have a quick look at the city while I had the chance. I took the bicycle again to try and avoid standing out, but the truth is that I stood out like a sore thumb as the only non- Arab to be seen. Most of the people I passed regarded me with mild curiosity, but then some bright spark decided to try and knock me off my bike with his car for a bit of entertainment. Realising that I was beginning to attract some very unwelcome attention, I cut my sightseeing trip short and headed back to the campsite.

When I was there I decided to try and fix a broken back light on the car with some superglue. One of the German lads wandered over and took over. He did a really thorough job, and when he finished I said "you fucking hero". This tickled him a lot. He and his mates were all into British punk music, and I spent a couple of hours regaling them with tales of all the bands I had seen play live in the '70s. They were big fans of "The Clash", "Siouxsie and the Banshees", "The Stranglers", and the like, and the fact that I had actually seen these bands play live in their heyday raised me in their estimation no end. They were a really nice bunch of lads, and it was a shame I couldn't join in their drinking games, but I was now 6 years sober, and those times were gone for me.

The next morning I wandered out from my tent and caught sight of Maurice and Anna talking a few yards away from me. As I approached them I suddenly felt the tears welling up inside me. The reality of what had happened to my mum suddenly hit me like a ton of bricks, and I couldn't stop the tears from cascading down my face as I walked toward them. Anna took me in her arms, gave me a big hug, and then began gently massaging my shoulders. All the pent-up emotion of the previous year came spilling out, and Anna held me until I had regained my composure.

I had been so isolated in my grief that the caring touch of another human being had triggered an outpouring of all the negative and painful feelings that had been building up ever since I had discovered my mum was terminally ill the previous December. Like everything else on this journey it had seemed perfectly natural to cry my eyes out in the arms of a total stranger, and once the moment had passed I felt surprisingly ok again, and a little relieved that I had found a safe outlet for the way I had been feeling about my mum.

The following day we set out to cross the Sahara Desert in our convoy of vehicles. Mohammed had somewhat surprisingly decided that my car was the strongest vehicle, (Peugeots have a great deal of kudos in that part of the World) so he decided that I should lead the convoy, and he would travel with me. Over the next couple of days he was to be my constant companion, and his mantra was always the same, "A la Gauche, A la Droit, or Doucement". These instructions were to avoid the numerous rocks and soft sand hazards that are found in the desert, and he would rattle them off in a barking, staccato, monologue as we made our way through the unforgiving landscape.

Being in the desert is like being at sea. There are no visible landmarks to navigate by, and the dunes resemble large waves that can make you totally invisible to anyone out of your direct line of sight. It was baking hot, and I struggled not to snap at Mohammed as he barked out his instructions. At one point we hit a long stretch of hard, dry, sand, and the vehicles fanned out, and drove abreast at 80 miles an hour. I had a Ramones tape on in the car, and the whole experience was slightly surreal as we drove towards the setting sun with "Suzie is a headbanger" blasting out of the car stereo.

There were numerous stops to dig the vehicles out of the sand, and as I was the only person in the group to have had the foresight to bring sand ladders, and a shovel, I was in constant demand, and I joked with the German lads that I was going to start renting out the shovel to them at an hourly rate.

One time when one of the German vehicles became stuck, Mohammed told me to press on along with one of the other cars.

After a while we stopped, and it became clear that we had lost the rest of the group. The light was just starting to fade, and Mohammed told me to retrace the route on my own, and go and find the rest of the group, while he waited with the other car that was with us. I had huge misgivings about doing this, but I relished the thought of being completely on my own in the middle of the Sahara Desert, so I put my fears to one side, and turned the car around. Before I set off I took a compass bearing, and boy was I glad I did.

I drove for about 20 minutes in what I thought was the direction we had come, and saw no vehicles. The huge dunes were like giant waves that blotted any direct line of sight, and I suddenly realised that I had no visual reference points whatsoever. It suddenly struck me that I was at huge risk of becoming lost in the desert, so I turned the car around again, took the opposite compass bearing to my outward journey, and headed off as quickly as I dared.

The light was fading fast, and I was beginning to panic. The seriousness of my situation hit me like a bucket of cold water. I knew that if I couldn't find the other vehicles, I was in a lot of trouble. I had about 16 gallons of water, and I knew that wouldn't last long in the heat of the desert. The chances of rescue were remote, as I was in a wilderness, in an underdeveloped country, that I was sure wouldn't want to waste valuable resources looking for an idiotic Westerner who had managed to get himself lost in the desert. I cursed Mohammed loudly for sending me back. What the fuck was he thinking of? Now we were all split up, and safety really hinged upon us all staying together.

It was almost dark, and I had almost given up hope, when I suddenly spotted the Germans. Thank God I was safe! Had I not had the sense to take the compass bearing before I set out I have little doubt that I could have been lost in the desert forever. It was a sobering thought, and I resolved never to just blindly follow someone's instructions again without carefully considering the potential consequences to myself first.

I had always had this mixture of fear, and respect, for anyone I perceived to be in a position of authority over me.. It dated back to my upbringing, where my Dad was the head of the household, and what he said was law. As an adult, this deference to perceived authority had almost cost me my life, so I made another mental note not to make the same mistake again.

Camping out in the desert that night was awesome. The sky was perfectly clear, and the stars seemed so close that you could reach out and touch them. Mohammed pointed out three stars in a line that pointed due north that you could navigate by, and the different constellations that were visible were spectacular. The night is cold in the desert, and I was glad of the thick sleeping bag that I had brought with me. I buried myself down in it, and enjoyed the feeling of warmth and security that it afforded me in the middle of that vast, untamed wilderness.

This was a far cry from living in the middle of Kings Cross, with all the noise, and the ever present sound of police, and ambulance sirens that seemed to be a continuous soundtrack to my life there, and it felt wonderful to lie in my sleeping bag, and soak up the almost perfect silence of the desert at night. I finally felt that I was free from all the petty little distractions that make up life as I had come to know it, and there was a sensation of almost timelessness as we camped out under the stars, in the vastness of the Sahara Desert.

In the morning we set off early, and the first part of the day was spent negotiating the many rocks that are a feature of the desert landscape. The driving was hard, and the boiling heat, and

Mohammed's staccato instructions, were beginning to take their toll on me. After one more barked order of "doucement, doucement", and when my hat flew out of the open passenger window, I finally had a mini-meltdown. I turned to Mohammed and yelled, "Shut the fuck up" at him. He kind of took it in his stride, and I decided that it was time to take a break. Maurice had been itching to drive ever since I had picked him up, and I decided to give him his chance. He leapt behind the wheel, and I got in the back of the car.

I was happy to let him put up with Mohammed for the next hundred miles or so, and as I relaxed in the back seat I watched the endless sea of sand pass by my window, as Mohammed plotted our course through the desert. After a while I swapped back with Maurice, and we were all rewarded with a spectacular sight. We had entered a part of the drive that involved 80 or so miles of driving straight along the beach, and this part of the desert had been designated as an area of natural conservation. As we sped along the sand thousands of Flamingos took off in front of us. It was a spectacular, and spellbinding, sight, as the birds flew off in all directions, and it brought home to me what a fantastic experience I was having.

We had to drive fast along this particular stretch of the beach as we only had a limited time before the tide would come in and trap our vehicles in the sand forever. Every now and then we would pass the skeleton of an old bus, or car, that hadn't been quick enough, and was now stuck in the sand for eternity. At one point we saw a huge ship that had somehow beached itself, and was now just a mass of rotting iron, lying on its side, in the shallows of the sea. These sights spurred us on, and we got to the end of the beach before the tide added us to its already quite sizeable collection of vehicles that hadn't been quick enough to escape its remorseless clutches.

It had been a memorable part of the journey. Camping in the desert, the Ramones sunset, the race against the tide, and the sight of the flying Flamingos, were all things that I was sure would stay in my memory long after the journey was over.

It was now nearing nightfall, and we all stopped to decide what to do. It was only another 25 miles or so to the end of the desert, and most of the group wanted to press on. I didn't relish driving in the dark, due to the many rocks we were encountering, but I was out-voted by the rest of the group, and we set off to drive the last stretch in the rapidly failing light. As we set off I felt a strong sense of foreboding. I didn't like driving in the dark at the best of times, due to my questionable night vision, but driving at night, in the desert, seemed to be asking for trouble. About 15 miles into the night drive my worst fears were realised. We had spent some 10 minutes negotiating a particularly tricky area of rocks, when there was a loud crack that seemed to come from the front of the car.

The Peugeot had come down off one particularly high rock, and had crashed nose first onto a smaller one. I got out to inspect the damage, and it didn't look good. Water was cascading out of the radiator, and it was obvious that I couldn't go any further under my own steam that day. I cursed the stupidity of the night time drive, and I cursed, and swore, at everyone, and everything else, under my breath. After about ten minutes I calmed down enough to consider my options. It didn't take long because the only option was to be towed by one of the other cars until we reached the campsite we were heading for in Nouakchott. I swallowed my pride and hooked the Peugeot to the back of one of the German's Mercedes, and I spent the last 25 miles of the desert journey being towed to our destination.

We arrived in the campsite in the dark, and I was still so angry I refused to talk to anyone. The rest of the party settled down in one of the large communal tents that were dotted around the site, and I resolved to sleep in the car. After a very uncomfortable hour or so I swallowed my pride again, and skulked into the tent with the others. This was Africa after all, and I was sure that a solution to my problems would be found in the morning. One thing I had learned in my previous trips to the continent was that Africans were geniuses at finding solutions to problems. It was an inbred resourcefulness, born of necessity, that came from living in an environment where the odds are stacked against you day, after day, and necessity has to be the mother of invention. I consoled myself with this thought, and finally went off to sleep safe in the knowledge that there would be someone on the campsite who would have an answer to my dilemma in the morning.

The next morning I rose early, and set to work on the car. Luckily I had brought plenty of tools with me, and I also had a tube of radiator sealant which would be the key to resolving my problem. I managed to get the radiator off, and I sealed the leak as best as I could. While I was doing this, Maurice and Anna informed me that they didn't want to hang around, so they would be leaving in one of the other vehicles as soon as they could. My German friends were on a pretty tight schedule as well, and with many apologies, they took their leave of me too, but before they left they gave Maurice and Anna a pretty hard time for leaving me in, what they considered to be, the lurch. I was on no time schedule at all, so I took stock and decided to just try and relax into my current situation.

I was right on the beach, and there were a few other people around to talk to, so I was in no danger of being lonely, or bored. When you are travelling it's generally not the locals that you need to be wary of, it's your fellow travellers who will rob you blind when you are not looking, so the fact that I was on my own again was of no account to me. I went for a swim in the Atlantic Ocean that lapped up against the edges of the campsite, and as I splashed around I reflected that on the whole things hadn't gone too badly up to this point. There were some big breaking waves where I was, and I longed to get past them to the open sea beyond.

My problem was solved when a local youth appeared, and showed me how to dive under the waves to get out to the deeper water that lay past them. The sun was getting hotter, the sea was getting warmer, and I could feel my strength building the further I got into my journey. This guy had a friend who was a mechanic, so for the cost of about a fiver my radiator was fitted nicely back in place, and I saved myself a hot sweaty afternoon trying to do it myself.

The lad who I had been swimming with suggested a night out with him at what passed for the local nightclub, so I delayed my departure, and decided to see what a Mauritanian nightclub was like. That evening we walked into what can only be described as a knocking shop for rich Arabs. I wasn't in there more than five minutes before I had a young African girl sitting on my knee. It felt a bit uncomfortable, but I had completely abandoned any kind of rules by now, so I let her sit there as I watched the local girls being approached by the large numbers of wealthy looking Arabs who frequented the place. The longer the girl sat there on my knee, the less able I felt to detach myself from the seeming inevitability of the situation, and as the night wore on she became more and more glued to my side.

As the nightclub began to empty at around 3am, I got up to leave, and the girl who had been sitting on my lap followed me through the door. It was obvious that in her mind some kind of deal had been made, and I wondered how I was going to extricate myself from what had become a very unwelcome situation. Luckily for me I spotted a taxi nearby, and after disentangling myself from her, and with a few oaths being hurled at my back, I flung myself into the back seat, and told the driver to take me back to the campsite.

The whole episode at the nightclub had left me feeling very uncomfortable, so I woke up early, packed my stuff, and left at sunrise, and continued south. The next stop was Rosso, a town on the Mauritanian/Senegalese border. I had been warned about this town, and strongly advised to avoid it, but it would take too much of a detour to go around it, so I decided to brazen it out. When I reached Rosso it was a shock to the system. It was absolutely teeming with humanity, and it was my first sight on this journey of Sub-Saharan Africa. The maelstrom of people was overwhelming after the solitude of the desert, and the shift from the generally quiet demeanour of the Arabic people that I had just left, to the raucous bustling Senegalese, was dramatic in the extreme. I immediately employed a "fixer" to get me through the potentially costly, and laborious, process of an African customs post, and for the princely sum of $20 I was ushered through, but not before I observed someone else having some serious problems.

A Dutchman was sitting in the cab of his big truck, which was besieged by what appeared to be a large number of very angry Africans. His fear, and arrogance, and their opportunism, had made for a dangerous combination, and he was getting the worst of it.

A large group of approximately twenty to thirty very muscular and angry looking Senegalese men were shouting and gesturing up at his cab, and one or two of them were trying to open his driver's door and drag him out onto the road. I made my way to the front of the mob, and called up to the Dutchman who by now was

33

looking far less arrogant and confident than he had been originally. I managed to persuade him to get down from his cab, and part with a few dollars to placate the angry mob, and after a while everyone began to calm down. This being done he was allowed to continue on his way, and I hoped he had learned a lesson from the experience.

From what I could see it was no use trying to stay aloof from the people whose countries you were travelling through, and attempting to do so only seemed to precipitate anger, and resentment. The Dutchman had had a narrow escape, and I hoped that he would show more empathy with the locals as he continued on his journey, otherwise he was in for a seriously rough ride.

While I was going through the customs post a French man approached me, and asked if I would carry him to Dakar. He offered to give me some money, and also to put me up in a nice hotel when we got there, but I was so glad to be on my own again in the car that I declined his offer. Who knows what adventures that would have led to had I accepted, but I was so relishing my own company again after having had Maurice and Anna in tow that I didn't like the idea of carrying another passenger so soon. Besides I had sensed that the Frenchman probably wouldn't have been the best company for me. He had seemed world-weary, and cynical, and I wondered what his purpose was in going to Dakar.

Chapter 4 – Fresh Pastures

I now felt that I was finally in the Africa of my imagination. The roads were red, and dusty, and the foliage was green, and lush. A few monkeys scampered in front of the car, and I stuck another tape on the stereo. This time it was "The Jam" that serenaded my arrival in Senegal. "Strange Town" blasted out of the speakers, as I drove along looking for signs to St Louis, on the way to Dakar. It was Christmas day 2002, and I was impatient to reach St Louis to find someone to share it with. After a few hours driving I pulled into the town.

Like Rosso had been, it was absolutely teeming with humanity. Everyone in town was celebrating the result of a big wrestling match. Wrestling is a big deal in Senegal, and the local hero "Bombardier", had just defeated his great rival "Tyson." This was much more important to the people of St Louis than the fact that it was Christmas, and I was pleased that I had arrived on such an auspicious day. Everywhere I looked people were celebrating, drinking, and having an almighty party in the streets. I rounded the corner in the main street and there right in front of me were Maurice and Anna. It was great to see them again, and it seemed the feeling was mutual as we all hugged each other, and got up to date with each- others news.

After a few minutes they threw their rucksacks in the back of the car, and jumped in with me. They knew of a beach resort nearby with some tourist hotels, so we set off in the general direction they had been given, and swapped stories about the last couple of days as we drove through the evening. As we neared the beach we hit some substantial sand dunes, and the car got stuck fast. We weren't able to dig it out, I couldn't shift it using the sand ladders,

and we laboured in vain to free the car for about an hour
Eventually, we had to concede defeat, so I threw the shovel to one
side, and we sat down in the sand. It was now night-time so as we
sat there we flicked on our torches, broke out some soft drinks,
and had an impromptu carol service by the side of the car. It was
another slightly surreal moment, and I really felt the true spirit of
Christmas as we sat there singing our carols in the middle of
nowhere, a long way from home.

After a little while a 4 wheel drive came by, and we negotiated with
the driver for a tow out of the sand. When the car was finally free
we followed him to one of the tourist hotels, and were just in time
to order dinner. After a fabulous feast of barracuda, and African
style rice, I put the tent up on the beach, had a final smoke for the
day, and lay back and reflected on the journey so far.

I had been almost killed in Casablanca by a lump of concrete
hurled off a bridge at me, I had been jumped by the two guys in
Tarfaya, I had driven straight into a sand drift on the approach to
the desert, and I had negotiated the toughest border I had ever
encountered at Rosso. I had also seen some spectacular sights, like
the flamingos in Mauritania, and the vast expanse of the Sahara
desert. I had swum through some big breakers in the Atlantic
Ocean, and met some wonderful and fascinating people. I was
only three weeks into my adventure, and there was a long way to
go. I couldn't wait to see what else was going to unfold on this
trip.

After breakfast the next morning I took in my surroundings. The
hotel was right on the beach, and there were a number of other
hotels dotted at various intervals along the sand. I went for a
wander, and bumped into a couple of Danish girls who had just
completed two years of V.S.O work in Senegal, and were now
spending a couple of weeks by the beach, before heading back

home. I was immediately struck by one of them. Her name was Ditte- Marie, and she was a Scandinavian Goddess.

Ditte Marie was about five foot ten inches tall, had beautiful blue eyes, bleached blonde hair, and a fabulous figure. We got chatting and I arranged to meet up with her and her friend that evening. In the meantime , and wanting something to do, I headed into the town to have a wander around. St Louis is an old French colonial town with wide avenues, and large dilapidated houses, and now I was in Sub- Saharan Africa I was really struck by the obvious poverty of the majority of the people that I saw. People were washing clothes in the river, and there were very few signs of material wealth. I was left pretty much alone in St. Louis, and I soaked up the sounds, and smells of this relic of a bygone era, as I wandered through its broad avenues, and dusty streets, while observing the day to day routines of the people that I passed.

As the afternoon wore on I returned to the hotel to keep my date with Ditte-Marie and her friend. I met up with them in the early evening, and there was obviously an attraction between myself and Ditte-Marie. As much as I was attracted to her, I knew in my heart of hearts that nothing could come of it, as I was still reeling from my mum's death, and my emotions were too fragile for any sort of intimate connection with anyone, even someone as drop dead gorgeous as her. I felt as though I was on a mission, and keeping the momentum going was the only way I could keep ahead of the grief that threatened to overwhelm me if I stayed in one place for too long.

It was a strange feeling as we spent the evening together, talking into the small hours, and all the time knowing that nothing could come of it. I eventually went to bed feeling rather confused over the strength of my attraction to this person I had only just met, but had pretty much poured out my heart to, and I finally fell into a fitful sleep full of dreams of Ditte Marie.

Early next morning saw me packing the car for the umpteenth time, and while I was doing this Ditte Marie appeared. She looked genuinely shocked to see that I was leaving and I really didn't know what to say to her. I mumbled a few things about having to continue my journey, gave her a peck on the cheek, said goodbye to Maurice and Anna again, and hurriedly bundled the last of my stuff into the back of the car. I jumped in the driver's seat and tore out on to the open road without looking back. It took a little while of driving for my mood to lighten but I was now on my way to Dakar, and after a few hours I arrived on the outskirts of the city.

I found myself in the red light district, and got myself a place to stay in a very run down guesthouse. It was a place where rooms were normally rented by the hour, but I negotiated a rate for the night, and after fending off the advances of some of the girls in the lobby, I made my way up to my room, and lay down on the large double bed inside. I had been able to park the car in the hotel's garage, which was just as well as all my Worldly goods were in it, and I didn't fancy having to carry them all up to my room for the night. I knew that if I had had to leave the car in the street, it would almost certainly be broken into, and I would have lost everything I possessed, so it was a blessing that this very unprepossessing hotel actually had its own garage.

Later I would go and have a look at Dakar, but for now, all I wanted to do was lie down and sleep. After a couple of hours of tossing, and turning, I gave up, and decided to go for a walk. Within minutes of leaving the hotel, I was approached by two men in plain clothes who claimed to be policemen, and asked to see my passport. I had been warned about this by some of my fellow travellers, so I was immediately suspicious of them. It was a pretty common ruse for people to pretend to be policemen to catch out naive travellers, so I pretended to be Russian, and kept shaking my head while they fired questions at me in English, French, Spanish, and every other language they thought that I might respond to. I kept replying with a constant stream of "Niets", and eventually I gave one last shake of my head and just walked off, praying under my breath that they wouldn't follow. They shouted after me but made no attempt to stop me, and I soon left them behind, and made my way towards the centre of town.

I didn't find much to see in Dakar that interested, or stimulated me. It was pretty obvious that there was a huge discrepancy between the rich, and the very poor, and the boutiques in the main streets were in stark contrast to the obvious poverty of the majority of people that I passed as I walked down its modern streets, and avenues. I sat down outside a small coffee shop, and decided to start practising my French with the waiter. My O' level French came back to me pretty well, and I enjoyed practising my pronunciation as I ordered my coffee, and food. I had always liked the French language, and I was finding that being in a French-speaking country was enabling me to start thinking in French.

It was really liberating for all that long forgotten knowledge to come flooding back to me, and I realised that I was a totally different person on this trip. I was toughening up mentally, and physically, and using skills that I had long since forgotten about, or never even realised that I had. I spent two nights in Dakar enjoying the comparative luxury of a bed to sleep in, and then I set off for the next leg of my journey to a place that was to become home for me for the next three years; The Gambia.

With no real idea of where I was going, I decided to cross into The Gambia about 200 miles down-river at a place called Basse. I had set off from Dakar quite late, and I arrived at the border just before nightfall. When I pulled up I was invited into a small room where a Senegalese army officer was sitting. He was a tall, elegant looking man, and as he was halfway through his dinner, he beckoned me to sit down opposite him while he finished his meal. Slightly warily I sat down in the chair facing him, and then was pleasantly surprised when he started to engage me in gentle, polite, conversation. He was very interested in my journey, and was extremely curious as to why I would undertake such a venture. I explained about the death of my mother, and my fascination for the African continent, and he asked me how I had found the Senegalese people so far. I told him that on my journey the majority of the people I had met had been gracious, and hospitable, and he seemed very pleased to hear this.

He found it hard to understand how I could leave all my family behind me in England, and he was very surprised that I wasn't married, and had no children, as he himself had two boys and two girls, and he was about the same age as me. He asked me to join him for dinner, but I declined as it was not long since I had eaten, and then he started to show me pictures of his family, and tell me about his life.

He was a charming and educated man, and I was glad to spend the next couple of hours in his company. It occurred to me that his was a very limited existence, stuck as he was in a tiny outpost in the middle of nowhere, and I was very happy that my arrival had seemed to mean so much to him, and that in a very short space of time we had struck up such a friendship. We chatted about the difference in our cultures, and about everything from cooking, to the merits of African footballers playing in European leagues. Eventually though I had to get going and I was sorry to take my leave of him. I promised that I would write to him when I eventually returned to England, and he escorted me through the

Senegalese side of the border. My passport was stamped, and then I passed through to the Gambian side of the customs post.

What a contrast! The Senegalese officer had seemed refined, and gentle, but the Gambians on first sight appeared to my Western eyes to be a bunch of savages! A number of soldiers were sitting around a large pot, and were scooping out balls of rice, and meat, with their hands, while shouting, and joking, with each other. They pretty much ignored me until one of them beckoned me over to join them at their meal. There was no way I was going to eat from a communal pot that people were dipping their hands into, and it must have been obvious from the look on my face that the idea appalled me. One of the soldiers noticed this, and made a great show of trying to entice me over to them, taking great delight in how uncomfortable it was obviously making me feel. The more I tried to politely decline his invitation, the more he made a great show of trying to invite me over. He was rolling up large balls of rice, and meat, and offering them to me in his outstretched hand, while laughing, and joking with his friends, as I became more, and more ill at ease. After what seemed like an age of trying not to offend this large, scary looking group, of unruly soldiers, my passport was stamped, a bribe was given, and I was ushered on to the police post on the other side of customs

A policeman approached the car, and asked me if I would be willing to take a soldier with me to Banjul, (the Gambian capital) as he had no way of getting there, and he had taken leave to see his family. By now it was night-time, and the thought of having a travelling companion appealed to me. The fact that he was a soldier was an added bonus, and I thought that having him with me would be useful if I had any problems. I also wanted to be nice, so I invited the soldier into the passenger seat, and we set off into the night.

41

My travelling companion was very large, heavily armed, and filled the front of the car with his presence. I put a Dire Straits tape on, and we drove through the night with "The Sultans of Swing" to keep us company. My companion was a great help for the road was truly appalling at times, and he showed me how to drive with one wheel on the verge, and the other in one of the deep ruts that ran along the middle of the road. I was driving through deep bush, in the middle of the night, with a large, scary looking, soldier in the car, and it felt great. I felt completely out of my element, and pleasantly uneasy, and I imagined how it must have been for the great Victorian explorers like Livingston and Mungo Park. Mungo Park had been murdered near here on his trip up The River Gambia in the 19th century, and although I knew that was extremely unlikely to happen to me, I still had that sense of being incredibly vulnerable, and it was exciting, and scary, at the same time.

After a while I noticed what seemed to be a large bushfire in the trees to our left. I pointed this out to the soldier, and he motioned me to stop. He disappeared into the forest, and I sat in the car and had a smoke. A few minutes later he re-appeared and got back in the car. Apparently some villagers had been burning some wood to make charcoal, and there was nothing to be alarmed about. I started talking to my companion about his job, and asked him what self- defence techniques they taught him in the army. I pulled over again, and so began an impromptu lesson in self-defence, in the middle of the night, deep in the heart of the Gambian bush.

He showed me how to defend myself against a knife attack, and where to strike someone to disable them as quickly, and efficiently, as possible I didn't know what was going to happen on this trip, so I made a mental note to store this knowledge for future reference in case I ever needed to put it into practice. This experience with the soldier made me feel that I was really beginning to connect to the people that I was meeting, and the country that I was now travelling through, and the experiences that I was beginning to have were as far removed from your average package holiday tourist as they could possibly be.

We continued on through the night until eventually, as we were approaching Banjul, the soldier motioned for me to stop the car, jumped out at the side of the road, saluted me, and disappeared into the darkness.

I had read before I set off from England that there was a tourist strip in The Gambia, and it was with visions of steak, and chips, swimming in my head that I drove the next 50 or so miles. Since the soldier had left the car I was feeling far less secure, as I travelled through the pitch black night. There were no street lights, and the moon was hidden by clouds, so the only light available was from the headlights of the car as they picked out strange shadows either side of the road in the surrounding forest. I had now been driving for 16 hours straight, and fatigue was beginning to set in. I thought I was seeing things when strange human-like shapes began to appear on either side of the car. It looked like something out of a post-apocalyptic film, and I found it hard to take in what I was seeing. There seemed to be an endless procession of people trudging in the direction I was approaching from, and as I drove past them I wondered what I was heading into.

I soon found out, and it was a welcome sight when I saw what appeared to be a number of restaurants, all brightly lit, and very inviting to my travel-weary eyes. I pulled up, and shouted out of the window to one of the diners. I had absolutely no idea of the context of where I was, and I must have looked like some kind of wild man to the people who I later found out had wandered out of their hotels to sample the main concentration of nightlife in The

43

Gambia. The car was covered in red dust, as was I, and I must have had a wild look in my eye after 16 hours of more or less continuous driving. The people sitting at their tables looked at me, and gently shook their heads, and I decided to head back toward the place where all those ghostly shadows seemed to be heading.

After driving a little while back the way I had come from, I saw a sign for a lodge, and pulled in. A very large Dutch youth, in his early twenties, took my money,(about £10 for the night), and showed me to my room. It was absolute luxury. There was air conditioning, and clean fresh sheets, on a large double bed, and I immediately lay down on it, and closed my eyes. It had been a long day, with some very hard driving, and I was asleep almost as soon as my head hit the pillow.

The next morning I got up, and decided to go for a mooch around, to try and get some idea of the lie of the land. I sauntered up to the main house, and was greeted by the same large youth that had let me in the night before. It turned out that he was looking after the place for his parents, who were on holiday in France, and he had the kind of attitude that was to become very familiar to me when I was talking to ex-pats in The Gambia. He described the Gambians as stupid, lazy, and dishonest, and I felt really uncomfortable in his company.

I wasn't on this journey to listen to other people's narrow-minded prejudices, but he then proceeded to tell me that he was a black belt in karate, and that I wouldn't stand a chance in a fight against him. I had no intentions of fighting him, but once again noted the effect that my presence had on the people around me. For whatever reason, this youth saw me as a threat, and his ego-driven paranoia insisted that I agree with everything he said. He did seem mildly dangerous in a way that only the truly disenfranchised can be, so I took my leave of him, and went for a cycle in the woods, behind the motel.

I too was slightly paranoid, and I took the large knife that my friend's Grandfather had given me, and hooked it on to my belt before I set off. I needn't have worried though because the cycle through the woods was magical. There were all kinds of birdlife in the branches above, and a number of monkeys flitted through the trees. I felt a tremendous sense of peace, and it felt at that moment that all my worries were thousands of miles away, and would stay there for the foreseeable future. I felt relaxed, and happy, and at that moment in time I didn't have a care in the World.

When I got back to the motel a young African girl was making up my room. She was very young (I guessed about 18), and extremely pretty. She seemed interested in me, which I found really flattering, and I chatted with her until the sun went down.

I had found out from the Dutchman that the place with all the restaurants was called Senegambia, and that that was the place where most of the nightlife in The Gambia was to be found. Compared to a lot of African countries The Gambia is very tourist orientated. It is the smallest country in mainland Africa, with an area of 10,689sq km, and has one of the highest population densities on the continent. The Senegambia strip was the focal point for all of the nightlife outside of the hotels, and I was really looking forward to having a slap up meal with all the things I hadn't eaten for the last month.

When the girl who worked at the lodge went home, I headed down to the strip, picked one of the quieter restaurants, and sat down, and ordered a plate of steak and chips. I thought the cost was incredibly reasonable, (about £4 for the meal with a soft drink) but I didn't know as I was eating it that that was the equivalent of a week's wages for most working Gambians at that time. Had I known this fact I don't think the food would have gone down quite so easily, but as it was I wolfed it down with gusto. While I was eating, a young girl plopped herself down in the seat opposite me. She said she was hungry, and asked me if I would get her something to eat. I ordered her a plate of chips, and wondered why the waiter looked so amused. The girl picked at her chips for a while, and then wandered off down the street.

When I finished my meal I decided that I could only spend two more nights at the motel, and when I left the restaurant I spotted a sign for a much cheaper place called "Soto Ba Koto," which was closer to town, and promised to be a more authentic experience.

The next day I woke up at 6am and stepped outside to get some early morning air. The maid who I had been talking to the day before was walking by, she came toward me, and before I knew what I was doing, I was pecking her on the cheek, and promising to meet her family the next day. When she went I took a long hard look at what I was doing. The girl was barely eighteen, and I was nearly forty. After my experience at the Mauritanian nightclub, I knew that it just wasn't on, so I decided to leave the motel that day. I packed the car, paid my bill, and set off for the place I had seen advertised the night before. The girl would no doubt be disappointed, but I sincerely hoped that it would be better for her in the long run if I just vanished from her life as suddenly as I had appeared in it.

"Soto Ba Koto" was situated in a village called Kololi, which was about half a mile from the beach, and after paying a week's rent in advance, which was roughly half what I had been paying at the lodge, I moved my stuff into one of the guest huts and decided to take a walk down to the seashore. As I walked, I took in my surroundings. At that time of year (early January) the climate was hot, and dry, and the streets, such as they were, were dusty, and scorched. Some ragged looking kids were having a game of football in the middle of the road, like you used to be able to do in Britain, and an old woman walked past carrying a load on her head, that looked far too heavy for her to manage. A few stray cats, and dogs, could be seen either lying in the shade of the various trees that lined the road, or making their way slowly down the street, as they searched for any scraps that they might be lucky enough to find.

I made my way down past the shops, and restaurants, in the Senegambia strip, and then walked through the Senegambia hotel, to the beach beyond. It was a large, sandy, beach, stretching about a mile and a half to my right, and as far as the eye could see to my left. All the activity seemed to be on my right, so I turned that way, and began making my way along the sand. As I walked, all manner of people approached me, offering to sell me everything from peanuts, to jewellery, and numerous girls would come down from their little huts at the edge of the beach, offering to give me a massage for a couple of hundred "Dalasis". I was feeling quite harangued by the time I finally reached a beach bar called "Kunte Kinte", obviously named after the slave featured in Alex Hayley's "Roots", and I asked an English couple if they would watch my stuff while I had a swim.

Five minutes later I was splashing around in the Atlantic Ocean again. The sea was considerably warmer than it had been in Morocco, and I looked forward to getting properly acquainted with it in the days to come. I stayed in the water for as long as I thought the English couple would look after my things, and then I dried myself off, and continued walking along the beach. At the far end of the beach I came across another beach bar, called "Leybato". This was a bit more upmarket than "Kunte Kinte", and it offered hammocks, and local food, for about 70pence a plate. I chose a dish called "Benechin", and was delighted when it arrived. It was a mixture of rice, fresh fish, hot peppers, sweet potato, and green tomatoes, and it was absolutely delicious. What a feast for 70 pence!

The only blot on proceedings came after I had finished my meal, and was sitting further along the beach, on my own, watching the waves rolling in from the Atlantic Ocean. As I sat there deep in thought about my mum, I was approached by a young Gambian lad. He started to talk to me, and I tried to make it clear that I wasn't in the mood for being hassled. I was feeling very upset about what had happened to my mum, and I just wanted to sit there and let the grief that I was feeling un-jumble itself, and allow me to get some kind of perspective on things.. I asked him repeatedly to leave me in peace, but he just wouldn't go, and eventually I exploded with a mixture of grief, and anger, and screamed "fuck off" at him, with tears rolling down my cheeks. The poor lad looked genuinely stunned at this response to a bit of pretty run of the mill hassling, but I was so immersed in my own feelings that I had very little empathy for him, and as he backed away I was left with the explosion of grief that he had triggered in me. I sat there for a while until I had calmed down, and then slowly made my way back along the beach, towards my lodgings in "Soto-ba-Koto."

The first impressions I had about the Gambians was that they were repressed, subdued, and basically a very gentle race of people. Their president had swept to power in a coup in 1994, and was now proving not to be as good for the country as had first been hoped that he would be. President Jammeh seemed to be a good example of the old adage, "that power corrupts, and absolute power corrupts absolutely". A few Gambians seemed to be doing all right for themselves, but the vast majority were living well below the breadline, while their president seemed to enjoy a life of unmitigated luxury.

As I had walked back along the beach after my meal, I'd felt a strong sense of wanting to do something good while I was here. I had limited resources, and limited time, but I had an immediate affinity for the Gambian people. They were the World's ultimate underdogs, and yet they seemed so friendly, and cheerful, in spite of their circumstances. I identified strongly with their struggle, as I had struggled so hard with my alcoholism, and I wanted to help them in any way I could. With these reflections running around my mind I went back to the lodge and decided to wash some clothes.

It was now dark, and the only place to do my washing was in a large, water-filled barrel, in the middle of the site. As I rinsed my clothes, I became aware of a girl sitting about ten metres away, who seemed to find the whole spectacle rather amusing. I smiled at her, and she laughingly asked me if I was German. Somewhat affronted I told her that I was British, and then she asked me what I was doing washing my clothes in the middle of the night. She still seemed to find the whole thing very amusing, and when she got up and left, another girl called Mary, who worked on the site, told me that the girl who had been quizzing me was called Adama, and that she was her cousin. Mary told me that Adama was a dancer in the Senegambia hotel, and that I should go down and see her perform the following night. For some strange reason Adama had made a real impression on me, and I told Mary that I would definitely go and watch her cousin dance the following day.

Chapter 5 – A New Beginning

The next evening duly came around, and I dutifully made my way down to the Senegambia Hotel to watch the show that Adama was dancing in. It was surprisingly good, with a mixture of Western, and traditional African dance, and even a comedy routine thrown in for good measure. Among the audience were a number of middle-aged British ladies, sitting down the front, who clapped, and cheered, certain of the male dancers. It occurred to me that the sex tourism thing applied to both sides of the gender spectrum, and that these extremely handsome, well-muscled, lads were just as appealing to the ranks of white middle-aged women, as the pretty young girls were to the men. To my Western eyes it seemed to be a pretty strange state of affairs, but then I was just in-country, and still extremely judgemental. After all, if these comparatively rich tourists were used by the locals as a means by which some of The World's wealth was redistributed it was all right by me. Anyway I was down there to see Adama, so it would be rather hypocritical of me to judge anyone else.

As I watched the dancing, I was struck by how professional Adama was. Her concentration was intense, and she never put a foot wrong. She was small, (about 5ft tall) in her early thirties, slim, and lithe, in a way that only dancers can be, and she had a bewitching way about her. She kept a smile on her face the whole way through her routine, and I was impressed. After the show, the dancers mingled with the audience, and Adama recognised me, and came over. I bought her a drink,(Fanta) and we sat awhile in the warm evening air. As time marched on I offered to walk her home, and we set off together through the bright moonlit night towards her home.

Adama lived in Kololi, near to the lodge I was staying in, and I walked her to her door. Much to my surprise she invited me in, and I stepped inside. Adama's home was basic to say the least. She lived in a small concrete room, with a corrugated iron roof, about 10ft long, by 10ft wide. There was no running water inside, and the electricity supply was sporadic to say the least. It was, however, immaculately tidy, and clean, and I ended up staying the night. It felt so natural to be with Adama. She had a wicked sense of humour, and in spite of having no formal education to speak of, she was one of the cleverest people I had ever met. In spite of all the odds against her, she was succeeding in being a single, independent woman, in a Third World country, and in a Muslim society, where such a thing was highly unusual, and generally frowned upon. I sensed that this woman had immense strength, and I was flattered that she had invited, and welcomed me, into her life. The bond between us was instant, and wonderful, and when we got up in the morning, we both knew that things would never be the same for either of us ever again

I spent the next few days on the beach during the day, and in Adama's small room, in the evenings. I couldn't remember the last time I'd felt so happy with life. I had no worries to speak of, and I was in love for the first time in many years. Adama suggested that I moved in with her, so I transferred all my stuff into her little room and took up residence. The first thing Adama had said to me when she invited me into her home was, "Me casa su casa," and the fact that she had so little, and was willing to share it with me, blew me away. I would try to repay this generosity by buying her a succession of little gifts, and she soon had quite a collection of silver necklaces to wear when she was dancing, in her shows, at The Senegambia Beach Hotel.

The compound that Adama lived in consisted of a big house, with three small huts along one side of the courtyard. There were three girls living in the huts, and nobody batted an eyelid when I moved in with Adama. Mariama lived at the end, with her little boy Diego, who was obviously the product of a union with a white man like me. Next to her was Haddy, who worked in the same dance troupe as Adama, and was in the room next to ours, and then there was myself, and Adama, who lived at the top end, next to the water pipe, at the end of the yard. The main house was occupied by a large family, with lots of children, and all in all we all lived together in relative harmony most of the time

I still had the travel bug, and one weekend I decided to go off and explore the south of the country. Driving here was totally different to driving in Europe. For instance there is only one set of traffic lights in the whole of The Gambia. Vehicles drive on the right, as in continental Europe, and consequently most vehicles are left-hand drive. There are numerous police checkpoints, and it pays to have your papers in order at all times. There is no automatic vehicle recognition system in the Gambia, and documents have to be produced on demand, so I always made sure that I had mine to hand wherever I went.

Early one Saturday morning I got myself properly organised, and I set off in the Peugeot, and headed down the main coastal road. According to the map this would take me through a place called "Bijilo," and on through "Gunjur," to a place called "Kartong," in the south of The Gambia. The road was surprisingly good in this part of the country, unlike the roads I had travelled along on my way into The Gambia, and it felt good to be on the move again. I had brought a "Steel Pulse" tape with me, and as I drove along the road I listened to the track "Man no sober," and shuddered as I remembered how my life had been before I had stopped drinking.

Here I was in Africa, sober, and living out my fantasy. Life was good, the sun was shining, God was in his Heaven, and everything was going to be all right. Money couldn't buy the way I was feeling at that time, and it was hard to believe how different my life was. Every now and then, as I was driving, I would come across a cow wandering along in the middle of the road. Adama called these beasts "The Kings", and as they disdainfully eyed the approaching Peugeot, I could see the regality of their indifference.

Kartong was only about thirty miles away, and it didn't take long to get there. Just before the town was a police checkpoint, so I slowed down, and the bored looking policeman waved me through. I knew that corruption was a big problem in West Africa, but on the whole the Gambians didn't seem to push it too far, and the small bribes that I occasionally gave, were given, and received, in good humour. I was to discover later on in my trip that not all of their neighbours were so trustworthy.

As I drove along, I passed a sign advertising, "The Boboi Beach Motel," and I turned off the main road, onto a dusty track, that disappeared into the bush. It led to a small complex of stone huts, with thatched roofs, and was presided over by a Scotsman, and his Gambian wife. For a small fee they allowed me to pitch my tent on the beach, and use the facilities on site, such as the shower block, and the many hammocks that were dotted around the place.

This really was away from everything, and for the next two days I swam in the warm ocean, and slept under the stars. The boys that worked at the camp took a shine to me, and when it was lunchtime, they invited me to eat with them from a large washing up bowl filled with rice, fish, and vegetables. We all sat around the bowl and dug in together. Most Gambians use their hands to eat, and are very skilled at rolling up the food into hard balls, which

53

they place into their mouths. I wasn't very good at this, so the boys, very kindly, let me use a spoon.

It dawned on me how quickly I was adapting to life in my new environment.. When I had first entered The Gambia, and had been confronted with a group of soldiers sharing a communal bowl of food, I had been revolted, but yet here I was now digging in like there was no tomorrow. I had always been pretty gung-ho, and that part of my character was serving me well here, as I enjoyed my lunchtime feasts, with the boys, who worked at the camp.

The Scotsman who owned the camp was called David, and he had first come to The Gambia about 20 years before, when he was still a young man, to do V.S.O work. He had met his wife Mariama in the local village, and they now had two children, Caroline who was 14, and Rory who was 12. They both lived in The Gambia with their mother, while David worked for U.N.I.C.E.F in various countries around Africa. When I got there he had just returned from Burundi, which he had had to leave in a hurry, after a death threat from the local rebels who had taken umbrage at his being there. David appeared to be very sanguine about the whole thing, and I was struck at the time what a contrast it was to my own rather insular way of dealing with things. The calmness he seemed to exude probably stemmed from many years of being connected to the African continent, and having to stay as diplomatic as possible in the face of extreme provocation. He also seemed to be possessed of a very calm basic nature, which I ,most definitely was not. David and Mariama were a lovely couple, who along with Rory and Caroline, and all the boys that worked at Boboi Beach, made me feel extremely welcome every time I turned up there, and I was to visit them many times while I was in The Gambia.

Just along from the motel was a sacred crocodile pool, and I decided to pay it a visit. It was deep in the bush, and on the day I went the crocodiles seemed to be on strike. One or two did surface momentarily, and I was invited to give some money to a wizened old lady, who I was told had special powers to protect me.

A lot of people in The Gambia believe in the power of Juju, and I had seen a lot of the boys on the beach, with various charms around their wrists. When I asked them about these charms, they swore they would protect them from anything from death by stabbing, to contracting serious illnesses. One boy even gave me a knife, and told me to stick it in him, believing that because of his charm the knife would simply bounce off.

Tempting as it had been at the time to put his faith in his charm to the test, I decided that it would almost certainly result in a trip to the local hospital for him, and some quite serious charges for me if I took up his offer, so I declined, and decided to let the mystique of Juju remain untested. I gave the old lady a few coins, and she gave me her blessing. In the circumstances, it seemed like a fair exchange.

After a couple of days at Boboi Beach, I decided to take a drive to the border with a region of Senegal called Casamance. I spotted a sign on the way for another guesthouse, and decided to take a look. This place was a big house, situated on a small hill, in the middle of some fields. It was owned, and run, by a larger than life character called Franco. Franco was an Italian man, in his late fifties, who was rumoured to be hiding from justice in Italy, and now lived out here, in the bush, in The Gambia.

The first thing I noticed about Franco was that he was extremely well- armed. There were rifles on the wall of his house, and he carried one pretty much everywhere he went. He reminded me a little of the Dutchman I had saved at the Rosso border post, and the Dutch youth at the lodge in Senegambia, and he seemed paranoid, excitable, and a bit of a control freak. I decided to stay a couple of nights for the experience, and moved into a small room at the back of the house.

Franco had a Gambian girl working for him called "Rocky", and I was immediately taken by her. Rocky was very attractive, and very spirited, and in any other society she would almost certainly have been able to make a living from her looks, but here she was forced to work for peanuts, for what I immediately suspected was a controlling, paranoid, miser. I really felt for Rocky, and had I not already met Adama I would have tried my best to do something for her. I was really physically attracted to her, and she seemed desperate for an escape route from the life that she was living. She asked me if I had a girlfriend, and I told her about Adama. We both realised that nothing could happen between us, and despite the obvious mutual attraction, we kept things on a platonic level.

We spent the long evenings at the house, playing cards together, and laughing at Franco, as he got angrier, and angrier for no reason. There was a bit of an atmosphere between the two of them, and I wondered if perhaps there was more to it than met the eye. Rocky, after all, was an extremely attractive girl, and Franco was a rich older man. He had what she wanted, and she had what he wanted. I wondered if somewhere along the line they had made a deal, and it had gone sour. Maybe me being there was making him jealous. I hoped so, because a girl like Rocky needed to be appreciated, and I felt that the fact that I was in the house, for whatever reason, had brought her to life again.

I stayed at Franco's for two nights, and while I was there I decided to go for a walk. The house was surrounded by fields, and I decided to walk through them, to the beach beyond. As I was walking, I passed some women working in the fields. They were probably doing the same work that their predecessors had done thousands of years ago, and it struck me that without western technology, and western systems, life went on the same as it always had done.

While I was walking, I watched where I put my feet. There are a lot of snakes in The Gambia, and although most of them will disappear as soon as they sense the vibrations from your footsteps, there is one particular type of snake that doesn't. This snake is the Puff Adder.

Puff Adders are short, and thick, and deliver enough toxins in their bite to kill a man stone dead within an hour. If a Puff Adder bites you, you have a very limited amount of time to get to a hospital before you are in serious trouble. Puff Adders are a stony, dusty, colour, and can be very difficult to spot, and if they bite you on the arm, or leg, you have a good chance of having the limb amputated if treatment isn't quick and efficient, assuming that you are lucky enough to survive of course.

Needless to say that knowing all this made me very careful, and my eyes scanned the ground constantly, as I picked my way very deliberately through the fields.

I was glad when I finally arrived at the beach, and saw the brilliant white sand laying out in front of me, and the bright blue sea stretching out to the horizon. There was not a soul to be seen anywhere, and I felt like I could have been on a desert island. I wanted to swim, and, as there was no-one around, I decided to go naked. I left my clothes in a little pile on the sand, and waded into the warm water. I had never swum naked before, and it was an incredibly liberating sensation as I let the waves gently massage my body, while I lay floating in the shallows. I stayed in the ocean for ages and luxuriated in my solitude. People pay thousands of pounds to swim on private beaches around the World, and I was enjoying the same luxury for free.

I seemed to have no fear on this journey. My mum's death had really brought home to me just how short a time we are on this planet for, and I was sure that if I behaved myself, then God, or the Spirit of the Universe, or whatever else you cared to call it, would look after me, and see that I came to no harm. I felt like my whole previous life had prepared me for this trip, and it was such a joy to be free. I'm not a religious man, but I fell to my knees on the sand, and thanked God for what I was experiencing. King's cross seemed like a million miles, and a thousand lifetimes ago, and all my worries, and grief, around my mum, seemed unable to touch me at that moment in time.

I took my leave of Franco, and Rocky, and decided to take a little drive to see what was beyond Kartong. About 400 metres past the village I came to a checkpoint in the road. Two bored looking soldiers sauntered over, and asked for my passport. They were big men, and heavily armed with what looked like sub-machine guns, and I was appropriately polite to them.

When I was dealing with soldiers in Africa I was always extremely polite. Apart from the fact that they carried guns, they were usually paid next to nothing, and had a pretty tough life, so I figured that the least I could do was show them some courtesy, and respect. Also the Gambian soldiers were, on the whole, pretty honest, and it was a pleasure not to be hassled for bribes every time I came into contact with them.

The soldiers looked at my passport, waved me on, and I drove for about another mile, until I came to a river. This was the natural border between The Gambia, and the Casamance region of Senegal. There were anti-government rebels in Casamance, and that was where Maurice and Anna had been headed. I had promised to meet them there, but I wanted to take Adama with me, so I had to wait for her to get the time off work before we would be able to go.

I was gradually getting used to the hot African sun now. It was extremely fierce, especially in the middle of the day, so although I loved the feel of the sun on my arms, and legs, I made sure that I always wore a hat if I was out in it for too long.

There were a few fishermen down by the river, and I motioned to them that I intended to go for a swim. One of them mimed a large pair of jaws, and I gathered from this that there were crocodiles in the water. I was feeling brave, but not that brave, and I decided to give it a miss. I was, quite rightly, very wary of crocodiles. They have been around since prehistoric times, and once a croc has you in his jaws it's usually game over. I had seen crocodiles before in Zimbabwe, and had even hit one on the head with a small stone, when it was lurking by the edge of the water. I figured that the crocodile race owed me some payback, and I wasn't in the mood to test the karma by going swimming with them.

After spending an hour or two at a small beach bar at the water's edge, I eventually turned the car around, and headed back to Kololi, and Adama. I had been away from her for five days, and was looking forward to seeing her again. Adama had an enormous amount of self- worth, and I don't think it crossed her mind for a second that I would be unfaithful to her. I thought about Rocky, and was glad that all I had done was befriend her.

I had been unfaithful to girlfriends in the past, (always when drunk) and the guilt, and depression, that followed these episodes,

59

had made me deeply regret them, so I was really glad that I had stayed true to Adama, and not cheated on her with Rocky. I got back in the early evening, on a night when Adama was dancing at the hotel, so I decided to go down and surprise her.

One of the major advantages of being white was that I could wander into any establishment completely unchallenged. Your average Gambian citizen couldn't do this, and I wondered how they dealt with the natural resentment that must have arisen from such an unfair situation. As I strolled into the Senegambia hotel, I enjoyed the anonymity of appearing to be just like all the other tourists staying there. I took my seat at the front of the stage, and watched the show unfold. Adama was brilliant as always, and as we were walking back to her room, later that night, I realised that fate had really put me with a strong woman. I had always been tossed around on the waves of life, but Adama had built her own boat, and sailed straight through the storms. I was a very lucky man to have found her, and I knew it.

I got into a routine after that. My weekdays were spent on the beach, and most of my evenings would find me heading to the Senegambia hotel, to watch Adama in her show, before we would take a leisurely stroll back through the village to our little room.

The day would generally start with an egg sandwich, liberally sprinkled with a Magi cube, and was always accompanied by a nice hot cup of tea. There were two types of bread that were used for the sandwich. It was either Senfoe, a light bread which the locals favoured, or Tapa Lapa, which was a heavy, doughy, bread, that the tourists preferred. I was gradually getting into the mindset that less is more, and although I liked the Tapa Lapa, I normally had the Senfoe.

Lunch would be had down at the beach, and was either an English type meal at "Kunte Kinte," or some local food at the Leybato beach bar. The local food was delicious, and was generally one of the following; Plassas (the leaves of a plant that had been mashed and stewed), Benechin (a combination of rice, vegetables fish and spices), Domoda (a peanut stew usually made with chicken), or Yassa which is a highly spiced chicken dish, served with onions, and chillies. All of these were served with rice, which is a staple food in this part of the World, and they were all equally fantastic.

For dinner I would either eat at a restaurant on the Senegambia strip, or I would meet up with Adama, and have some of, "Anne Marie's chicken", which was cooked, not surprisingly, by a woman called Anne-Marie, who worked at the Soto- Ba- Koto camp. Anne-Marie's chicken was a real treat, and it was good to see that Adama,, a self- confessed poor eater, would gobble it up enthusiastically every time we had it.

It was an idyllic time for me. I would spend my days on the beach, diving in and out of the warm Atlantic Ocean, and the nights at home, in our little room, with Adama, where we would spend the evening hours playing cards, chatting, and listening to music.

When I was down at the beach one day, I got talking to one of the many fishermen who worked there, taking tourists out fishing, on the nearby reef. His name was Farmara, and he offered to take me out swimming with him. I am a very strong swimmer, but not knowing the local sea I had been afraid to venture too far out on my own, so when he offered to go with me I jumped at the chance.

We set off, and powered through the surf, to the open sea beyond. We swam for a good half an hour, and when I looked back the shore was way off in the distance. The current wasn't too strong, and Farmara and I were both good swimmers, so we carried on a bit further. I was quite happy to carry on indefinitely, but, after a while, my companion suggested we headed back, so we turned around, and struck out for land.

It was another liberating experience. All too often I had felt prevented from doing things through fear of the unknown, and now I had swum out to sea once, I knew I would be able to do it whenever the fancy took me. When we got back I started chatting with Farmara, and he told me a terrible story.

Apparently, three months before I had arrived in The Gambia, there had been a terrible tragedy at sea. The Joola ferry had been transporting pilgrims from Ziginchour, (in Casamance) to Dakar, when it went down in heavy seas, 20 miles off the Gambian coast. 1900 souls had been on board, and 1800 of those people had perished when the ferry went down. There had been many women, and children, on board, and they had all gone down with the ship.

I couldn't remember seeing anything about this in the English press before I had left the UK, and I was shocked at the sheer scale of the disaster. It could be that I had been so preoccupied with what was happening to my mum that I hadn't noticed, or it could have been that, like with so many things that happened in Africa, the Worlds press had only paid it a passing reference. More people died on the Joola ferry than had perished on The Titanic, and while The Titanic is still etched on people's consciousness 100 years later, most of my contemporaries have never heard of The Joola Ferry.

Farmara told me that for months after the accident bodies had been regularly washed up on the beaches, and he himself had helped to dispose of many of them. It had obviously had a very bad effect on him, and not for the first time I wondered why the people of this vast continent had to endure so much suffering. If God did indeed have a plan, this was a piece of it that I just couldn't understand, so I tried to put it out of my mind, and stay concerned with my own day to day experiences.

Chapter 6 – Casamance and Haddy

After hanging around on the beach for a while, I finally agreed on a price with Farmara to go fishing, and the next day we set off for the reef. I had never been fishing before, as it had always seemed such a sedentary pastime to me, but I went with an open mind, and was delighted by the experience.

I discovered that I had excellent sea legs, and the first thing I caught in my life was a huge Moray eel. The fish came thick, and fast, after that, and by the time we had finished for the day I had caught Butterfish, Zebra Fish, Red Snapper, the aforementioned eel, and a couple of Catfish. What a delight it was to go fishing in a place that yielded such a good catch! I took pictures and proudly showed them to a distinctly unimpressed Adama later that evening. The only fish that she was interested in were the ones that she got from the market for our evening meal, and I realised that this was one passion we weren't destined to share.

I got into the habit of going fishing pretty regularly after that, and I met some more of the boys that made their living down there on the beach. The beaches were patrolled by soldiers, and as the fishermen were doing something legitimate they were left in peace. The rest of the local youths were kept off the beach so they wouldn't be a nuisance to the tourists, but periodically the ones who had found a way down there were rounded up by the soldiers, taken to a detention camp, and beaten with heavy sticks to dissuade them from venturing there again.

The beaches had long been troubled by a phenomenon called "Bumsters." These "Bumsters" were young lads who made their living by hustling down on the beach, and the Gambian authorities were terrified that their continued activities would have a detrimental effect on the tourist industry, so their answer was to round them up, and beat them. I could see that these youths were an annoyance to the tourists, but it also seemed to me that it was yet another example of Africans being denied their basic human rights, and this time by their own Government.

The soldiers had little option but to do what they were told, the real blame lay with President Jammeh's government, who prized the tourist dollars above the welfare of their own people. For my money, the best part of The Gambia WAS the beach, and ordinary people could not enjoy it in peace. It was a dreadful situation for the young Gambian lads who often had no other way of making any money, and it seemed like a really screwed up state of affairs to me.

Another thing that was most noticeable to me on the beach were the amount of elderly white ladies with handsome, muscular, young, Gambian men. At first I found the sight strange, and quite repulsive. These, after all, were women in their 60's, with boys in their twenties, but after a while I realised that it did not behove me to stand in judgement

Both parties were obviously getting something from the arrangement. The boys were no doubt getting financial benefits, and the ladies were buying the illusion that they were still desirable to young men. Again I came to the conclusion that if it kept the distribution of wealth flowing the right way I was all for it.

Occasionally you would see one of these women appear on T.V. in the UK claiming that they had been deceived into believing that these young boys had been in love with them. From where I was standing it just looked like a convenient transaction, youth for money, and anything else was just an attempt by the women to justify their vanity, and naivety, when the arrangement almost invariably collapsed when they brought the boys back to their own countries.

By now I had learned a couple of phrases in the local Woolof dialect. The first one was "Mema Suma jamma," which roughly translated means, "give me some peace," and the other one was, "Topa so- sa- sahola," which meant "mind your own business." Occasionally I would use one of these phrases when I was being hassled on the beach, and the ladies that sold fruit to the tourists used to tease me mercilessly, shouting out "Topa So" whenever they saw me coming.

It was good-natured banter, and I played my part enthusiastically. Being included in their daily banter made me feel accepted in a way that no amount of giving money away ever could, and I was gradually beginning to feel like I belonged down there on the beach. They call The Gambia "The Smiling Coast," and one of the favourite sayings there is that "It's nice to be nice". I suppose that when you have got very little, being nice is one of the few things that is still an option, and I have to say that the majority of people I met there were really good at it.

I had now eschewed the comfort of the tourist beach bars, and spent most of my time hanging out with the fishermen down on the beach. We wiled our days away by swapping information, playing football, and trying to get people to go for trips on the boats. As well as Farmara, I had made a host of new friends among the fishermen. They accepted me into their World, and I would repay this kindness by sometimes buying lunch for everyone. For the same price as a meal at one of the tourist bars, I could buy lunch for five or six people, and I felt in a very privileged position. After a while I soon discovered that it really was "nice to be nice", and I was in a position to be nice nearly every day. The effect this had on my mental health was

66

tremendous. There is nothing as good as being good to others to make you feel good about yourself, and I felt fantastic nearly all of the time.

Since I had been for my swim with Farmara, I had got into the habit of swimming at least half a mile out to sea every day, and this coupled with a diet that consisted of mainly fish, rice, and vegetables, meant that my body, and mind, were getting honed into shape all the time. I had so much energy in spite of the intense heat, and I felt alive in a way I had never felt before.

I didn't miss anything about home. I didn't miss baked beans, or brown sauce, or tomato ketchup. I didn't miss fish and chips on a Friday night, or a roast dinner on a Sunday. I didn't miss the daily diet of television soaps, and strangest of all I didn't miss any of the people I had left behind in Britain. I had thrown myself into the local culture so fully that the things that had first appeared so strange were now becoming my normality, and it surprised, and delighted, me that I had adapted so quickly to my new environment.

It was around this time that I had a brainwave of sorts. Since I had been with Adama I had realised how lucky I had been to meet her, and my brain raced ahead, and came to the conclusion that in order to minimise possible future hassles, we should get married as soon as possible. Adama agreed, so we went up to the registry office in Banjul, and set a date for March 17, which is, of course, St Patrick's Day.

I had never been married before, but Adama had, and she had a son from a previous marriage that lived with his father in The Gambia. She had no contact with her little boy, but she carried a picture of him around in her wallet wherever she went, and it was obviously a source of great pain for her. Her little boy's name was

Francis, and I prayed that one day I would be able to help her be reunited with him.

After we had arranged the wedding I suggested to Adama that we take a trip to find Maurice, and Anna, my two hitchhiking friends who had gone to Casamance. Adama took some time off work, and we set off. It was now beginning to get very hot, so I made sure the car was properly topped up with water, and I carried some spare water, and fuel, in my jerry cans.

The road to Casamance was reasonably good, and we got there in about nine hours. When we arrived we went to a roadside bar for some soft drinks, and started to watch a small black and white television that someone had set up on the bar. The Gambian president, President Jammeh, was waxing lyrical on the station that it was showing, and the patrons of the bar were almost falling off their chairs laughing at him. Adama and I got a serious fit of the giggles, and joined in the merciless ribbing of the Gambian president.

Adama, in particular, was really enjoying being able to be so openly scathing of her country's leader, as in The Gambia being so openly critical of someone who was basically a dictator could have got her in a lot of trouble, and it was good to see her cutting loose at him.

When we had finally stopped laughing, we asked if anyone knew where the white Rasta was staying, and one of the bar's customers told us that he thought he was living in the bush close by. After a bit of exploring we found them living in an old dilapidated house, in the middle of the bush, not far from the sea. They were delighted to see me, and Anna in particular seemed slightly surprised that I had Adama with me.

68

Maurice was spending his days working with the local Rasta community, and Anna was basically playing house while she had the opportunity. We pitched our tent in the yard, and then I went for a walk down to the beach, leaving Adama chatting with Anna. It was yet another stretch of beautiful deserted coastline, with not a soul to be seen, and I plunged into the sea. It was really noticeable how the further south I got, the warmer the sea became. I had swum in the sea in Morocco, Mauritania, and The Gambia, and now that I was in Cassamance the sea felt even more like a warm bath.

That night Adama and I made love. Being out there in the middle of the bush had heightened both our senses, and our lovemaking was intense, and electric. There was something about being completely free that made every experience, and every feeling, so much more memorable, and Adama and I's lovemaking had topped the lot for me, on the trip so far

Later on in the night I came awake to the sounds of noises in the bush outside our tent. I had been a little bit nervous of coming to Casamance, as I knew it was a rebel stronghold for the people who wanted independence from Senegal, and I was a bit fearful that there may be people there who might think it was a god idea to kidnap me. I was worried that the noises I heard could be someone creeping up on our camp, so I slipped quietly out of the tent, and took the big knife that I had brought with me from the U.K. I hid in the bushes, and waited.

My senses were tuned in to the bush around me, and my hearing became ultra- sharp as I strained my ears to pick up any sounds coming from the area surrounding our tent. I could feel my heart pounding in my chest, and I didn't know what I would do if anything happened, but I felt incredibly calm, and I just sat and waited. After about half an hour of waiting in the dark, with my

69

knife to hand, I returned to the tent. The noises had stopped, and I felt safe again.

My senses remained super alert for quite a while afterwards, and I eventually dropped off back to sleep after an hour or two. It could have been a stray monkey, or some other small creature that had made the noise, but I had no way of knowing this, and I figured that it was better to be safe than sorry.

It was an awesome experience that I was having in West Africa, and the more I did, the more I felt that I was becoming part of the fabric of life there. With our western ways, and devices, we cut ourselves off from our basic survival instincts, and as life becomes more comfortable, and safe, we lose the power of our senses to protect us, because they are just not needed any more. Out there in the bush it was life on life's terms, and I loved it. I felt like the person I had always been meant to be, and I was relishing every second I spent away from the homogenised, sanitised, and controlled existence I had left behind me back in The U.K.

In the morning I said nothing to Adama about what I thought I had heard the night before, and we set about cooking some eggs, on the open fire, in the middle of the camp. We didn't do much for the next few days apart from sit around chatting, exploring the local bush, and going for long swims in the beautiful warm blue ocean, as we enjoyed our time in Cassamance.

The days drifted by in a happy daze, and before we knew it, it was time for Adama, and I, to return to Kololi. We had stayed with Maurice and Anna for five days, and I was sad to say goodbye, knowing in all likelihood that I would probably never see them again. I knew that I was not very good at keeping in touch with people I met on my travels, as seeing people again in normal circumstances never recaptured the magic of experiences you shared with them while travelling, so I had learned that some people were best kept in the memory.

I stored Maurice and Anna in my memory banks, wished them a fond farewell, and we set off on our journey back to The Gambia. When we got back home, Adama's family, and friends, were delighted to see us safe, and well. They knew the risks of travelling to Casamance, and the fact that I had brought Adama back in one piece made them very happy.

That night we celebrated in her friend's compound, and told stories about our adventure. I was beginning to feel a real affection for the day to day people I met in the village. It was lovely to see "the lazy man", as Adama had christened him, outside his shop, and all the little children playing football in the middle of the road. The dusty streets of Kololi were rapidly becoming my new home, and it felt good to be back.

We had been back about three days, when we were woken one morning by the sound of extremely loud music outside our bedroom window. Adama's friend, and fellow dancer, "Haddy," lived in the room next to us, and before I had come on the scene they had done lots of things together. I sensed that Haddy wanted to be noticed, and I felt myself getting angrier, and angrier. I don't generally feel at my best in the mornings, and the cacophony outside our bedroom window pushed me over the edge

I stormed outside, and saw a large "ghetto blaster" perched on Haddy's windowsill, blaring out the noisy Senegalese music that she was so fond of, so I reached up, and turned the volume down. Haddy came flying out of her room, and turned it back up again. We then had a five-minute tussle for control, during which threats were made on both sides. By now a large crowd had gathered, and Adama had come outside, and was arguing with her best friend.

71

I suddenly realised what a complete idiot I was being. A few days before some youths had thrown a few stones at me over the compound wall while mockingly calling me "Toubab". I had thrown the stones back at them, and because I felt marginalised by my colour, I felt that I always had to take an aggressive stance to protect myself. It had been answered in kind by Haddy, and the situation had escalated to a point where it had almost got completely out of hand.

For all I knew Haddy was probably just letting off a bit of steam by listening to her music, and I, true to form, had completely overreacted. Again I felt a bit ashamed of myself, and quickly apologised to her.

Gambians tend not to hold on to arguments for long, and once it was done, it was done. We made up, and soon we were all laughing, and joking with each other again. Most Gambian people are very poor, and poor people tend to live in the instant. Arguments are explosive, and soon forgotten, because generally speaking people have more important things to worry about, like putting food on the table each day, or looking after a sick family member, so petty squabbles are not held on to for long.

I was to have a few experiences like this while I was in The Gambia, because I was living in a way that didn't shield me from the harsh realities of people's lives, and my own, sometimes volatile nature, would occasionally bring me into conflict with them.

There are two main seasons in The Gambia, the dry season, and the rainy season. The dry season lasts from November till July, and as it progresses it gets hotter, and hotter, until the rains come at the beginning of July. We were now at the end of February, with the days at a constant 90 degrees, and the cool nights in the mid-sixties. It was too hot for me to stay in the village during the day, so every morning I'd make my pilgrimage down to the beach, where the sea breezes made it slightly more bearable.

I would normally walk, and on the way I would be greeted many times by the locals, who would shout out "hello Toubab" as I passed them. I found out that white people were called "Toubab" because when the British colonised this part of the world the soldiers would often bargain by offering the sum of two bob, for goods, and services, offered by the locals. Ever since then all white people had been referred to as "Toubabs," and most of the time it was just an innocent greeting. There were occasions when it wasn't however, and unfortunately I was always very quick to pick up on this.

On Sundays I would rest, and stay in the compound. During these times I would write, and I soon had an impressive collection of Gambian children's stories, with titles like, "Snow in The Gambia," and "The Friendly Crocodile." On these days Adama would go to her friend's compound, and bring me a lunch of fish, rice, and vegetables.

I still loved the food that I was eating every day, and I couldn't get enough of it. The diet was having a fantastic effect on my health, and I was losing weight all the time. The lack of fat, and sugar, in my diet meant that I was healthier than I had ever been, and I knew now why the Gambian men had such fantastic physiques. Their diet, combined with hard physical labour, gave them bodies that the middle-aged Toubab ladies drooled over. I still had a way to go to catch up with them, but I was heading in the right direction, and it felt good to feel the fat dropping of my body daily, and my muscles hardening up as the regular swimming, and helping out down on the beach, began to have an effect.

By now I had found a mechanic to do some work on the car. His name was Omar, and he had a small yard just off the main Senegambia highway. The first time I took the car to him I was astonished when a gang of children appeared, and began dismantling my engine. The youngest of these boys was eight years old, and Omar explained to me that the best way for them to learn was by on the job training. Anything that wasn't too difficult, he let them do, and as a result they eventually became skilled mechanics like him.

I really took a shine to these kids, and whenever I had work done on the car I would make sure that they got a few hundred dalasis. They were paid a pittance, and I really hoped that the money would put food on their family's tables for a day or two at least.

I couldn't believe how good Omar was at his job. With virtually no equipment, and in searing hot temperatures, and the most basic conditions, he got the jobs done in half the time a fully equipped British garage would have taken, and with far less messing around. I didn't negotiate too hard with Omar, as he always quoted me a more than fair price, and it was always about a fifth of what it would have cost me to get the work done in the UK.

I was becoming more and more impressed with the people of The Gambia. They worked ridiculously long hours, in mostly appalling conditions, and they generally took home less than £4 a week. Added to this, they rarely complained, and nearly always tried to look after any family less well off than themselves. Their stoicism seemed incredible to my spoiled European eyes, and I admired them greatly. It was an absolute joy to be able to be slightly generous from time to time, and I gave away a lot of money to some very deserving cases while I was there.

Chapter 7 – Marriage, Rambo, and Guinea Bissau

Before I knew it, the day of my marriage to Adama had arrived. It was now the middle of March, and I had been in The Gambia for about ten weeks. Adama and I got married on March 17th, 2003, and we asked our taxi driver, Fillijee, to be a witness at the ceremony. It was just myself, Adama, and Fillijee, at the registry office in Banjul, and, during the vows, Adama promised to take me as her "lovely wedded husband,", an endearing mistake that made us both laugh.

Later that evening we had a small party at her friend's compound to celebrate. Some lads brought a sound system along, and we bought a dozen crates of soft drinks. During the party I went on the roof of the compound, and watched the people dancing below. I felt that distance from events that had plagued me all my life, and I said a silent prayer that I was doing the right thing for myself and Adama, so soon after meeting each other.

The party went on into the night, and eventually, I escorted a very happy, and tired Adama, back to our little room in Kololi. As we curled up together as man and wife, in our little corrugated room for the rest of the night, it felt to me that I had never lived in King's Cross, and the life that I was now living was what it was always meant to have been. The next morning we were woken early by a girl called Aiwa, from Adama's friend's compound, knocking on our door, and calling out "wake up Mr and Mrs Coughlin." My name was a source of great amusement to her, and as she rasped, and spluttered, in her attempts to pronounce it correctly, Adama and I collapsed in a heap of giggles, and teased her mercilessly, until she eventually almost got it right.

Around this time I had become aware of a dog in the village called Rambo. Rambo was flea-bitten, riddled with worms, and covered in scars from fighting other dogs. He looked like a combination of a labrador, and a corgi, and he had been given his nickname because he was fearless, and tough, and rarely lost a fight. Rambo had used to belong to an Englishman, but when the Englishman went home he had been left to fend for himself.

What we consider to be domestic animals in England have a really tough time in countries like The Gambia. The people are generally so poor that they can't afford the luxury of sentiment when it comes to animals. They have enough trouble feeding their children to worry about the welfare of stray cats, and dogs, and added to this is the fact that rabies is a constant risk, so any wild cat or dog is seen as a potential carrier. Stones are thrown at dogs to keep them away, and most of the unfortunate four- legged creatures I saw had crescent-shaped scars on their heads, where they had been hit by some kind of projectile.

Much to the dismay of Adama, I became quite fond of Rambo, and I used to feed him regularly with tins of corned beef, bought from "The Lazy Man," in the corner shop. Rambo soon started to follow me when I went to the beach in the mornings, and I would have to resort to all kinds of subterfuge to shake him off. The village was separated from the beach by the main road, and I used to worry that in trying to follow me he would get run over, or that he would get stoned by people who weren't familiar with him.

Most of the time I managed to shake him off before the main road, but occasionally he would make it as far as the Senegambia Hotel, and then the security guards at the entrance would unceremoniously send him packing.

Rambo soon began putting on weight, and looking much healthier, and happier, but the fleas that he would bring along with him meant that Adama categorically banned him from setting foot in our room. This didn't stop me from sometimes letting him come in when Adama wasn't around, but I was careful not to let him get too comfortable, and I made sure that all traces of him had been eliminated before Adama got home from work.

I knew that ultimately I couldn't save Rambo, but I decided to do what I could, when I could, to help him survive. This was my attitude with many of the people I met on a daily basis as well. I couldn't change anyone's life forever, but I could make things slightly easier for them while I was there, and I tried to help whenever I could.

Soon another Englishman moved into one of the huts in the compound. He was a lorry driver from the North of England, on a kind of sabbatical, and he had moved in with Mariama, and her son Diego. Beyond saying hello occasionally when we passed each other, I never really bothered myself with him. We were both in the Gambia to escape from our lives in England, and the last thing either of us wanted was to be reminded of what we had left behind.

This man had a dog called Castle, and he had learned the Woolof word for "come here". He seemed to spend his entire time calling out" Kai Castle! Kai Castle!" to his dog, and when he left after a couple of months I was very happy. He had met one of the prostitutes on the Senegambia strip, and he moved out of Mariama's to be with her. I saw them together once, and she was definitely a striking looking woman, but she looked hard, and materialistic, to me, and I felt sorry for Mariama, and Diego. Mariama only referred to him on one occasion to me after he left her, and what she said was, "big man, big fool."

Mariama was a lovely person, and I couldn't help agreeing with her. I guess that he had been her potential ticket out of the daily poverty for her, and her son, and she was disappointed, and angry, that he had let her down, and moved on so quickly.

Even though nearly all of the people I met made the best of it, their lives seemed almost unimaginably hard to my spoiled European eyes. How they kept their cheerfulness in the face of such daily hardship was an incredible, and inspiring, thing to witness. Sometimes it made me sad, but I made sure I kept moving, so I wasn't overwhelmed by it. A rolling stone gathers no moss, so I kept pretty mobile during the days, and I think my toughness, and my sometimes uncompromising nature, kept me from a lot of unnecessary hassle as well.

There was a massive rubbish tip just off the main road that skirted Kololi, and many people eked out a daily existence by foraging for things in it. It was hard to imagine anything worthwhile being thrown away in a country as poor as The Gambia, but these people seemed to find something to make it worth the effort, and when I walked past the tip, on my way to the beach, I would see an army of human scavengers picking their way through the mountain of reeking detritus.

To some extent I had to harden myself to the poverty, or it would have overwhelmed me, but from time to time, when I was able, I would give people some money to help them for that day.

There were so many odds stacked against the majority of people in The Gambia that I often wondered how they tolerated it as well as they did. There was the poverty, the lack of opportunities, and the relentless climate to contend with. There was malaria, which, without being able to afford antimalarials, was a constant danger, especially to young children, and the elderly. There was the oppression from their own government, and there was the constant reminder, provided by the tourists, that not everyone in the world faced such overwhelming difficulties. The size of the problem was heart-breaking to observe, and must have been so much worse to be stuck in it.

Although I was living pretty much as an African would, I had advantages that they could only dream of. I had a bit of money, which can buy you out of most types of trouble, and through being a British citizen, I had the ultimate, "get out of jail free" card, if things got too hard for me. If it all got too much I could just jump on a plane, and come back to the UK, with its incredible, and much-maligned, National Health Service, and a benefits system which kept me from the kind of abject poverty that most Gambians had to endure, even if they were lucky enough to have a job.

Poverty for the majority of Gambians wasn't about not being able to afford a new T.V, or whether or not to have chicken, or lamb, for dinner, it was about the daily struggle to get enough to eat, and not to succumb to the many illnesses, and diseases, that they couldn't afford the medicines to treat.

I still had the exploring bug, and it was about this time that I decided that Adama, and I, should take a trip further into West Africa. I still had the trusty Peugeot, and that was to be our mode of transport for our next adventure. Adama had an uncle who lived in Guinea Bissau, so we decided to pay him a surprise visit. To get there we had to drive through Casamance, in Southern Senegal, and then through most of Guinea Bissau, to get to his home in the capital Bissau. I readied the car, delved into the selection of maps I had brought with me from England, and we set off early one morning, at the beginning of April.

The first part of the journey went smoothly, and it was great fun throwing handfuls of sweets out of the car window, for the children that we saw, as we drove through the many villages, but the problems started as soon as we hit the Guinea Bissau border. I had to pay a large tax to be allowed to enter the country, and then once we were across the border we hit a series of checkpoints every two, or three hundred, yards, and at each one I was asked for a bribe to let us pass through. I had no choice but to pay, and the small amount of cash I had for the trip dwindled alarmingly each time we were relieved of another "Deux cent Francs".

Adama was particularly outraged at our treatment, at the hands of her fellow Africans, and she had a hard job containing herself each time we were stopped. Sometimes she just couldn't prevent herself from giving the hapless soldiers a severe tongue lashing. These, after all, were her "brothers and sisters," extorting money from us just because she was travelling with a "Toubab," and she was as outraged as I was at the unfair treatment that we were receiving, at the hands of the soldiers.

I wasn't entirely comfortable when she was haranguing them, as they were big, strong looking men, who carried automatic weapons, but her vehemence seemed to shame them into silence most of the time, even if it didn't stop them from insisting on the bribe.

Due to the poor roads, and the number of times that we were stopped, night fell while we were still in the middle of Guinea Bissau. There was no lighting, and my night vision has never been the best, so when the road appeared to swing suddenly to the left I followed it around a slight bend, and up to the top of a small hill. Without realising it, I had somehow lost the main road, and taken an unwitting detour, straight to the middle of a camp full of soldiers, and police.

As we pulled up a great commotion ensued, and guns were drawn, and pointed at the car. For a few seconds we were completely at the mercy of our new captors, but when the excitement died down, and they realised that I had merely taken a wrong turn, the opportunity for extortion occurred to them, and we were ordered to drive back down to the proper checkpoint, and await further instructions.

We were left to cool our heels for the best part of an hour, and then a group of policemen came down, and started harassing us. This was too much for Adama, and she totally let fly at them. One of the policewomen shone a torch in her face, so Adama took her own torch and shone it straight back in the face of her tormentor saying, " if you torch me, I will torch you". If it hadn't been so serious it would have been almost comical, but all hell broke loose again, and once more we found ourselves looking into the barrels of several pistols that were pointed directly at us. Adama wouldn't let it lie though, and she started calling the soldiers, and police, thieves and beggars, and saying that they should be ashamed of themselves.

This seemed to take the wind out of their sails a bit, but they then insisted on seeing our passports. I refused to hand them over, and instead offered a copy of an international driving license that I had brought with me. This seemed to satisfy them, so they took it with them, and told us to stay where we were. They then wandered back up the hill, and left us to our thoughts.

We sat there for another hour, and nothing seemed to be happening, so I made an executive decision. I told Adama to fasten herself in, and then simply sped away from the checkpoint. Knowing how unlikely it was that they had any effective means of communication, I rightly guessed that no-one ahead would be dispatched to block our route, but I did worry that we would be shot at as I drove away, so we both kept our heads low as the car moved forward.

Thankfully the sound of gunfire didn't accompany us as we sped off into the darkness, but it was a nervous few seconds for both of us as we accelerated away, and disappeared into the night The only problem that I could really envisage was that we would almost certainly have to pass through the same checkpoint on the way back, but that was so far in the future, that I dismissed it from my thoughts, and we carried on through the night towards the capital.

We arrived in Bissau at around midnight, and started looking for somewhere to spend the night. After driving around for the best part of an hour, we eventually found a cheap hotel, and went up to our room on the second floor. It was stiflingly hot here, much hotter than The Gambia, and the room was tatty, boiling, and not very well ventilated. I couldn't stand it, so I left Adama in the room, and went down to sleep in the car. It wasn't much better in the car, but at least I could keep the windows open, and I managed to get one or two hours of fitful sleep.

The next day Adama emerged from an equally uncomfortable night, and we went in search of her uncle. He worked in the port authority, and turned out to be an easy man to find, so we spent the afternoon with him and his family, in a rather hot, and very busy, house. I asked him if he knew a safe place to leave the car for a couple of days. And he said that we could leave it at his workplace, so the next day I drove it down to the port, and left it in the hopefully safe hands of Adama's uncle.

There are some islands off the coast of Guinea Bissau called "The Archipelago dos Bijagos, and I really wanted to see them while I was there, so the following morning we headed down to the docks, and took a very overcrowded ferry to one of the larger islands, called "Bolama.." I had insisted on bringing the tent with us, and I also carried two jerry cans to be filled with water, so we would be able to spend some time basically living on a desert island.

When we got to Bolama we found a local market, and bought fruit, vegetables, and rice, to sustain us for two or three days, and I packed them into the small rucksack that I had brought along with me. I felt that we made a formidable pair. I was as gung-ho as anything, and Adama was tough in the way only Africans can be tough. Between us we should be able to cope with anything that three days living on a desert island could throw at us, and I felt confident that we'd be just fine.

We hitched a ride on the back of an open truck, and set off to find our beach for the next few days. It was incredibly hot, and the fierce looking youth, that was riding on the back of the truck with us, hacked at the branches overhanging the road, with a large machete, as we drove through the bush.

After an hour or two the boy signalled to us that it was time to get off, so we unloaded our stuff, and started to carry it down a small track, to the beach beyond. We had to make two or three trips, as the water was heavy to carry, and the heat was like a furnace, but when we finally got everything down to the beach, we set up our tent, and started to think about what we were going to have for dinner. We boiled up some rice on the primus stove we had brought with us, and added a couple of tins of corned beef, purchased from "the lazy man," before we had left The Gambia.

Although it was a very basic meal, as we sat under the stars, on our own private beach, it tasted absolutely heavenly. Afterwards Adama cut up a couple of mangos, (there is a particular way of cutting mangos that I never got the hang of) and we finished off with a nice cup of tea, sitting together, on the sand, outside our tent.

In the morning I decided to test the sea. I had been warned that the waters surrounding these islands were teeming with stingrays, and sharks, so I took a big stick with me when I went in. It was true, there were thousands of stingrays in the water, and I beat a path through them with my stick, as I tried to get out of the shallows.

I really didn't want to get spiked by one of these creatures. Stingrays have a barbed spike, which goes through flesh very easily, but is almost impossible to get out. It is notoriously agonising to be zapped by a stingray, and to be a victim would almost certainly involve a couple of days of excruciating pain, before being able to get to a hospital to have the barb removed.

Knowing all this didn't stop me from continuing my advance through the water, until I got out deep enough to have a decent swim, and it was a relief when I was far enough out not to have to worry about putting my feet down. I didn't see any sharks, but then again I guess you only see them when they have decided that you are on the menu, and after about fifteen minutes I decided to head back to land.

Coming back in was a nerve-racking experience. I was terrified of putting my leading foot down on a stingray, and the waves were knocking me all over the place, while I decided where to put my feet. I still had the stick, and I beat the water furiously in front of me, to drive any stingrays away. After a nerve-wracking few minutes, I negotiated my way through the shallows, and I finally arrived triumphantly back on the beach.

While I was on this trip, I had the constant need to confront danger, and I think that it still had something to do with the death of my mum. Death confused, and frightened me, and I felt the constant urge to fly in the face of it. It was almost as if I was shaking my fist at God, and saying, "go on then, I dare you!". It was a dangerous game to play, but at the time I wasn't aware that that was what I was doing.

Adama, for her part, was along for the ride, and although I didn't mean to put her in danger, I wanted to do things with her, and that meant that she would be exposed to the same risks as me sometimes. I guess she had a choice, and she must have decided that it was worth the risk to spend time with the crazy "Toubab" that she had married, so in her own inimitable way she came along, said very little, and observed everything

We spent three days and nights on our desert island, washing in the water from the jerry cans, and sleeping under the stars at night. There was only one blip. We were having a disagreement about something, and I kicked a training shoe in Adama's direction. It was just like the infamous Alex Ferguson incident, when he kicked a boot at David Beckham. The shoe flew straight up and hit Adama in the face. I was absolutely mortified, I hadn't intended to hit her, and I immediately apologised. Adama was really angry, but eventually she calmed down, and we made up.

Once again I had let the volatile part of my nature get the better of me, and I had been lucky that the consequences hadn't been more severe, and that Adama was prepared to forgive and forget.

In the mornings I would go for long runs along the golden, sandy, beach that ran in both directions, to the front of our tent. I tried to get Adama to come with me, but as she put it, "Mr Coughlin I am not a runner," so I would end up going on my own for my early morning exercise.

We had three idyllic days there on our private beach, and when our meagre supplies had finally dwindled to nothing, we gathered up what was left of our stuff, and headed down the beach to a pick up point, that we had agreed with the truck driver that had brought us there. He took us back to the ferry port, and we got on the boat back to the mainland.

The ferry was even more overcrowded than it had been on the outward journey, and as I looked at the mass of humanity packed onto the listing deck, I thought of the Joola ferry disaster, and said yet another silent prayer to whatever it was that had brought me safely this far on my journey. It was truly frightening to see just how many people had been packed onto its decks, but the ferry just about creaked, and groaned, its way back to Bissau, and when we eventually disembarked, we hunted down Adama's uncle, and were reunited with the car.

Thankfully the Peugeot was still in one piece, and after saying our goodbyes to Adama's uncle, and his family, we decided to spend one last night in Bissau, before heading for home.

Guinea Bissau had had a civil war in 1998/99, and as we wandered around the city that evening there was a vibrancy to the place that seemed to combine a sense of relief, and celebration, at the same time. The citizens were bright, and energetic, and as we wandered past the various food stalls, and open-air restaurants, nobody stopped to disturb, or bother us. The people we saw seemed intent only on enjoying themselves, and we blended into the landscape as one would, in say, London, or Paris.

We bought some chicken, cooked on a small barbeque in front of us, and spent a good few hours exploring, and soaking up the atmosphere. The sights, and smells, and energy of the city, entranced us both, and we finally turned in just before midnight. This time I elected to sleep in the room with Adama, and maybe because I was slightly more acclimatised than when we had first arrived, although the room felt stuffy, it didn't feel as overwhelmingly stifling as before.

In the morning we set off on the journey back to The Gambia. The drive was pretty uneventful, and apart from passing a couple of long since abandoned T54 tanks, left over from the Civil War, nothing of note happened until we reached the checkpoint that we had been stopped at on the way into Guinea Bissau. We were immediately recognised, and there was pandemonium as the soldiers ordered us out of the car at gunpoint.

This time I knew there was no point in arguing. We were totally outnumbered, and there was no way that they were going to run the risk of us driving off again. I was forced to hand over the car keys, and both of our passports, and we were hauled in front of the commanding officer. We had pretty much run out of money by this point, so I wasn't even able to resort to bribery to resolve the situation. It wasn't a good state of affairs. I had angered them by driving off before, I had no money to pay any bribes, and Adama and I were completely at the mercy of these large scary looking men with guns.

I had a big bag of lollipops in the car, and I got them out and started handing them out to everyone. This amused them no end, and when I started to juggle with three lollipops, their mood completely softened. They let us go, and as I drove off I reflected that it was showing a little humility that had saved us, and allowed us to carry on, on our journey back to The Gambia

Those soldiers weren't bad men, they were just very bored, and very poor, and bringing it down to the level of lollipops had broken the barriers down between us. African soldiers, on the whole, get a pretty bad press, but I found them to be more than receptive to being shown some respect, and humility. Most African values are about family, and humanity, and even the most corrupt soldiers will respond if you appeal to this part of their nature. At the end of the day the lollipops had done the trick, when all else had failed.

The next problem we hit was a checkpoint in southern Senegal. I didn't have enough money left to pay the bribe that I was asked for, and the soldiers were adamant that they wouldn't let us proceed unless I did. It was the middle of the day, it was scorching hot, and the soldiers had all the time in the world, but I was determined not to let them get to me this time.

I noticed a game of football being played behind the border post, so I wandered over, and asked if I could join in. I left Adama sitting in the shade, and threw myself into the match. This would show the soldiers how unconcerned I was, I thought. I played for a good eighty minutes, and when I was just about exhausted the soldiers called me over. They had realised that they weren't going to get any money, so they grudgingly handed back our passport ,and sent us on our way.

The final problem we hit was the Gambian border post. The bribes I had had to pay on the journey into Guinea Bissau had left us seriously short of cash, and I didn't have enough money to pay the import taxes to get back into the country. The Gambian border guards would not believe that a rich "Toubab" had run out of money, and they were convinced that I was lying to them. They were adamant that they would not let us back into The Gambia if I didn't pay them what was due, and I knew that no amount of cajoling on my part was going to change their minds.

Luckily I had brought some spare parts for the car with us, and I managed to sell a starter motor, to somebody hanging around at the border post, for enough money to gain us entrance back into the country.

After we left the border post, another two hours of driving saw us finally arrive back home in Kololi. We got a fantastic reception from all of Adama's friends, and family. They were so happy to see us back in one piece, and I was really touched at the depth of feeling that was shown to us. I really felt that Adama's friends, and family, had become my friends, and family, and I now felt totally at home, living in this little African village, with my adopted African family, and friends.

Chapter 8 – The Gambia versus Senegal

By now I had got to know most of the fishermen who worked off the main beach, taking tourists out to the reef. There was Farmara, who I've already mentioned, a guy called James, and a Rastafarian called Solomon. They all worked together, using a boat that was owned by a Dutchman, who used to visit the Gambia three or four times a year, to collect his share of the earnings. This group of fishermen was completed by a few young lads, who did the more mundane tasks, and got a much smaller share of the profits.

Farmara was a Gambian, who was well muscled, and stocky. James was originally from Senegal. He was tall, and broad-shouldered, and his muscled physique reminded me of polished mahogany. Solomon was the coolest character of the three of them. He was a dedicated Rastafarian, and he was suitably laid-back, and also had the obligatory muscly physique. They were all tough individuals, and very different in temperament, but they seemed to co-exist quite nicely down on the beach, and they welcomed me into their circle with virtually no drama.

I wiled away my days on the beach with this trio, and also took to trying to coach football to one of the lads who helped out on the boat, in a bid to improve his already quite startling football skills. This lad was called Abu, and I got on with him like a house on fire. We both loved football, and after kicking a ball around for hours at a time, we would then sit down and spend an equal amount of time discussing the merits of Manchester United, Barcelona, and Real Madrid, and trying our best to set the football world to rights.

I was now starting to have a totally different outlook on life. I lived with Africans, I ate with Africans, and the only real contact I had with white people was when I was trying to persuade them to go out on my friend's boat. The old fat "Toubab" ladies no longer looked strange to me, as they walked past on the arms of fit, young, Gambian men. I was becoming less and less judgemental, and more and more open to the philosophy of it being "nice to be nice." The lifestyle that had been so alien to me when I first arrived, was now becoming normal, and I realised that I liked being around people all the time, especially the Gambians, who were so friendly, and unaffected.

When I had lived in London, I had spent most of my time alone, in my flat, in Kings Cross, and now that I was here, I could barely get a second to myself if I wanted to. I found it almost impossible not to be generous, as I had so much compared to the people I was mixing with each day. It wasn't a big deal to give money to the beggars, and the feeling that it gave me inside more than compensated for the financial loss. Adama, to her eternal credit, never asked me for a thing, and added to this was the fact that I was living rent-free in her room. All in all I was having a fantastic time, and I never wanted it to end.

Adama's mum lived in a little village, in the south of The Gambia, called Sifoe, and we decided that it was time we visited her, to let her know that we had married, and Adama now had a "Toubab" husband. We drove down there one weekend, and as I pulled up on a patch of ground next to a large compound, the car was besieged by a gang of children who had been playing football nearby. For some reason I decided to tell them that my name was Jimmy, and as we made our way to the door we were accompanied by the sound of "Jimmy, Jimmy" being shouted out by all of the kids.

Inside Adama's mum's compound were three or four buildings, with corrugated roofs, and in the garden were mango, lemon, and cashew trees. Adama's Dad had passed away many years before, and he had a large grave, in the grounds of the compound, just to the front of the main house. It was an imposing grave, and it really felt that he was still there, and in some way still watching over his family, as he lay there beneath the ground.

Adama's Dad had had four wives, and they were all still alive, and living in the same compound. When we pulled up they were all at the front of the house doing their domestic chores. One of them was sifting the rice grains ready for the main meal of the day, another was sweeping the yard with an old besom, and the other two were washing clothes, in a big tub, in the middle of the yard

Adama introduced me to her birth mother, and I was taken aback at how warmly she welcomed me into her family. She was probably in her late fifties, and her face was gentle, and kind. She spoke no English, but her manner left me in no doubt that she was pleased to see me, and she gave me the feeling of being entirely embraced by her, and welcomed as her daughter's new husband.

While we were in Sifoe, Adama took me on a walk in the surrounding countryside. She pointed out the different plants, and flowers, and introduced me to the mighty Baobab tree that is found in this part of the World. The Baobab tree is often referred to as the upside-down tree, because its branches look like the roots of the tree sticking up in the air. It bears a fruit, which when mashed, and supplemented with a little sugar, makes a delicious drink, and I became quite fond of this while I was in The Gambia.

She told me to watch where I put my feet, in case there were any Puff adders lying on the path, and she pointed out a hornet's nest, which we took a large detour to avoid. After a while we stopped, and slept under the branches of a large Baobab tree, and then we wandered back to the compound where we sat and ate some of the delicious benechin that had been prepared while we had been on our walk.

I was humbled again by how simply Adama's family lived out here in the countryside. This was another world again from life at the beachside, and I felt like I had stepped back in time three hundred years.

Adama then took me to a local Still, where I watched as palm wine was being made. She told me that there were many alcoholics in her village, and that when they came to her mother's compound to beg, they were always made to eat something, before they were given any palm wine. Alcoholics are given a pretty rough time by most folk, where I had come from, but these good people tried to do what they could for them, and given my own struggles, it touched me greatly that they cared enough to do this.

Adama told me that most of the time her mother got by on very little, and in harvest time she depended on the small revenue that she got from selling her mangos, lemons, and cashews. It was a hard life, and it struck me that, since the death of Adama's Dad, the farm had struggled, and many of the fields had been left uncultivated, and bare.

I thought, at the time, that it was severely underestimated by many westerners, with their comfortable lives, and judgemental attitudes, just how tough life can be for people in this part of the world. It seemed that, at times, everything conspired to defeat their best efforts to improve their situation. Quite often the climate would be against them, an outbreak of disease could suddenly occur, or their own politicians would, through personal greed, leave the majority of the people in abject poverty, while they themselves enjoyed a life of unmitigated luxury. If, by a combination of hard work, and resourcefulness, they did manage to get anything together, it would quite often be ruined by some type of unforeseen natural disaster, or an outbreak of social, and economic unrest.

Aside from all this there was the ever present threat of malaria, and the lack of money for the medicine to treat it, to contend with. The longer I was in The Gambia, the more my respect for these people was growing. The only way out of poverty for most Gambians was through education, and even if they were lucky enough to afford to get that, there was no guarantee that there would be anything for them at the end of their studies.

When dusk started to fall, we said goodbye to Adama's mum, and drove back to Kololi. When we got back, we stopped at "Soto Ba Koto," and got some of Anne-Marie's chicken, to round off what had been an almost perfect day. We washed the chicken down with some fizzy drinks that we had bought from "The Lazy Man," Malta for me, and Fanta, as usual, for Adama.

Malta was a local drink, which was basically vitamin B in a bottle. I drank it mainly because I liked the taste of it, but also because I had been told that mosquitoes can't abide the smell of vitamin B, and drinking Malta meant that you sweated it out through your pores. I had abandoned taking any recognised form of antimalarials, since the Amoxicillin I had brought with me, had caused a severe sensitivity to sunlight, that had resulted in me spending one night sleeping with my hands in a bucket of water, to soothe the burns on them, that had been caused by the sun reacting with that particular drug.

I pretty much took my chances with malaria for the rest of the time I was in The Gambia, and this was something, which later on, would have some quite serious consequences for me.

It was now April in The Gambia, and there was a big African Nations football match coming up. The Gambia had done well so far in the competition, and their next two matches were against their biggest rivals, and close neighbours, Senegal. The Gambia was in the grip of football fever, and the first match was to be played at the Gambian national football stadium.

I had never been to a football match in Africa before, and I was soon caught up in the enthusiasm that was sweeping the country. I bought six tickets for the match, so as well as myself, and Adama, we were joined by Filijee, the taxi driver who had been the best man at our wedding, and three of Adama's friends, who also wanted to come along.

On the day of the game, the atmosphere in The Gambia was electric. We made our way to the stadium, at least two hours before kick-off, and mingled in with the gangs of Gambian youths, who were milling around outside. There were Gambian flags everywhere, and I got a tremendous sense of the immense national pride that people were feeling. Gambians don't generally have much to shout about most of the time, so this football match was a huge deal to them, and now, as I felt like one of them, it was to me as well.

Senegal's football team is pretty well known on the world stage, having participated, and done reasonably well, in a couple of World cups, and the Gambian team were rank underdogs for this fixture. However there was a real feeling among the Gambians that this time they would finally be able to put one over on their illustrious neighbours, and as the kick-off approached, the excitement built to a crescendo.

It was all standing where we were, and we were packed in tightly together. We all had our shirts off, (except Adama), and we were waving Gambian flags, and singing "we are hot, very, very, hot, BONFIRE, " at the top of our voices. I so wanted The Gambia to win this match, to bring some happiness to these tough, and long-suffering people, and when the game kicked off the Gambian team started well.

The match was well contested, and there were chances at both ends. The much-maligned "El Hadj Diouf," once of Liverpool fame, had a good chance for Senegal, and the Gambian keeper made some good saves to keep the score at nil-nil, when the half-time whistle was blown. The second half was as tight as the first, again there were chances at both ends, and when the final whistle blew, with the score at 0-0, the Gambians celebrated as if they had won, which in a way they had.

The Gambia is the smallest country on the mainland continent of Africa, and they had held the mighty Senegal to a goalless draw. It was similar to an England- Scotland game, in what it meant to the Gambians. Like the Scots, the Gambians are always the underdogs in these fixtures, and like the Scots, any result against their dominant, and more powerful neighbours, was cause for huge celebration. They may not have won, but more importantly they hadn't been beaten, and for the most part the Gambian crowd was elated.

With my Dad being Scottish, I had always supported Scotland as a child, so I easily identified with the underdogs of my adopted African country, and I walked away from the stadium happy, and optimistic about their chances in the second leg.

The return match was in Dakar in a fortnight,, and there was no way that I was going to miss it. The two weeks went by very quickly, and I decided to drive to Dakar, for the second leg. In the car were myself, Adama, Solomon, and Farmara. We tied a huge

Gambian flag to the top of the car, and set off to drive to Dakar, the long way round, by crossing the border upriver at Basse, the way I had entered The Gambia, when I first arrived in the country.

The first part of the journey was long, and tiring. The road into the interior was terrible, and I quite often had to drive with one wheel on the top of the huge ruts in the road, like my hitchhiking soldier had shown me how to do all those months before, on my way into The Gambia. By the time we reached the border 6 hours later, we were all tired, and in need of some refreshments. Adama went out and bought us all some pastries, and fizzy drinks, and we sat in the hot sun for a while, as we ate, and drank our fill.

The car was drawing a lot of attention, thanks to the flag on the roof, and all the Gambians that went past were wishing us luck, and predicting a good result for the Gambian team. Farmara was revelling in the attention, and enjoying himself immensely, and it was really nice to see him so animated, and excited, with something to shout about for once.

We got through the border without any problems, and set out on the next stage of the journey. The drive to Dakar took us through a town called Kaolac, and when we reached there, the car drew lots more attention. The Senegalese we passed were all highly amused at our flag, and they were shouting things at us as we drove by. Farmara was hanging out the window, shouting "cinq-zero" at the top of his voice, as a prediction of the score, and the Senegalese were laughing their heads off at his audacity, and optimism. We finally reached Dakar at about 9pm, and I decided to drive to the stadium to check it out.

I had noticed, as we drove through the outskirts of Dakar, that the reactions to our flag were becoming more, and more, hostile, but we kept it flying as we drove into the stadium car park. I drove towards a large group of youths standing by the main gates, and the sight of us, with our Gambian flag, immediately provoked a scary reaction. Bottles, and stones, were hurled at the car, and the mob surged towards us.

I slammed the car into reverse, and backed up about two hundred yards. Why I didn't just keep going I'll never know, but I decided to stop the car, and get out. I had noticed that the majority of the mob were youths of only about sixteen, or seventeen, years old, and for some insane reason I had decided to make a stand. Farmara got out and joined me, and Solomon, and Adama, quite sensibly stayed in the car.

Farmara and I were arguing over who should have the piece of piping, that I kept in the door- well, and then I had the rather obvious thought that it would probably be a good idea to take the flag off the roof. We dismantled our flag, and stood there for about ten minutes, in what felt like an almost choreographed show of defiance, but the mob didn't come any closer, so we got back in the car, and drove off.

I don't know why I got out of the car, instead of just driving away from the situation, but I suspect that once again my stupid pride, and arrogance, had got the better of me, and I hadn't wanted to lose face by running away. I didn't know how many chances this continent was going to give me, but I was beginning to feel like I was certainly pushing my luck.

I drove us to the motel, in the red light district, that I had stayed in when I had stopped off in Dakar, on my way to The Gambia, and Adama, and I, got a room, while Solomon, and Farmara, elected to sleep in the car. This was a happy arrangement for me, as it meant that the car would be well looked after as we slept, and Solomon, and Farmara, seemed to be more than happy with their choice of accommodation for the night.

After a decent night's sleep, (for Adama and me at least) we set off in the morning, back to the stadium we had had such a close call at the night before. We got there at about 11am, and the atmosphere was already building nicely for the match. Most of the Gambian supporters had already arrived, and we joined them at our end of the stadium.

The Gambian supporters were really hyped up for the game, and there was a crazy, slightly edgy, atmosphere, starting to develop among them. I got pretty carried away with it all, and I threw myself into the middle of them, ripped off my shirt, and joined in the tribal dancing. I felt passionately for my adopted country, and shaven-headed, and bare-torsoed, I ran up and down, waving a Gambian flag, and screaming at the top of my lungs.

After a while we began taunting the Senegalese fans as they walked past, and the atmosphere began to grow volatile. We had high hopes for this match, as we all believed that this time the Gambian team could pull off a famous victory, and at about 1pm we made our way into the stadium, and joined the ranks of Gambian fans that were already present at our end of the ground.

There were a lot of Gambian fans that had made the tricky journey to Dakar, and we were all packed in together, on the terraces, at one end of the ground. It was a seething cauldron of colour, and noise, as the teams made their way out to the pitch, just before three o' clock, and as the game kicked off, I was still running up and down at the back of the terrace, waving my Gambian flag, and taunting Senegalese fans.

From the first whistle the Senegalese team were a different proposition to what they had been in the game in Banjul. The Gambian players struggled to contain them, and it wasn't too long before Senegal took the lead. A great groan went up from our end of the stadium, as the goal went in, but we regrouped quickly, and redoubled our efforts at encouraging our team. The Senegalese scored again just before halftime, and we spent the break singing, and encouraging each other, that it was still possible to get a result. Our faith was rewarded in the 60th[th] minute, when The Gambia got a goal back. Our end of the stadium went completely crazy, as the ball crossed the line, and we ran up and down, hugging each other, and punching the air with delight.

This triggered a response from the Senegalese fans closest to our enclosure, and missiles soon began raining down on us. I noticed large rocks, and heavy cans falling among our ranks, and the rage that I felt was shared by many of my fellow supporters. Senegal scored again as the match drew to a close, but by now my focus was completely on what was happening in the crowd.

The Gambian fans had responded to the Senegalese by throwing the missiles back at them, and the Senegalese army poured into the ground to separate the two groups of supporters. They created a no- man's land between the Senegalese, and us, and the missiles that the Senegalese fans were throwing were no longer reaching us. I had almost lost the plot by this point, and I ran towards the Senegalese fans, waving my flag, and shouting at them.

A soldier blocked my path, and very calmly told me that what I was doing was not helping matters. This took the wind out of my sails somewhat, so I stopped what I was doing, and made my way back to where Adama and Solomon were standing, at the back of the terracing. Farmara had been involved in the thick of the trouble, and he was still missing when I got back, so it was just the three of us who were left.

At the final whistle all hell broke loose. The final score was 3-1 to Senegal, but that was quickly driven from our minds by the events unfolding inside, and outside, the stadium. As soon as the match had finished, the Senegalese fans had poured out of the ground, and taken up position behind us, on the outside of the stadium. They started to break up pieces of concrete, and were raining them down on our heads from their positions outside. It was a long way to throw, but many of the missiles were finding their way over the wall, and landing amongst us.

At the same time that this was going on, fighting was breaking out in the stands to our left, and it appeared as if the Senegalese troops were randomly laying into the Gambian fans inside the ground. I saw one poor man being mercilessly beaten by several soldiers, and it angered, and incensed me.

By now we had crouched down behind the wall, at the back of the terracing, to gain some protection from the missiles that were raining down on our heads, and the thought occurred to me that the people, on the ground, throwing the missiles, were in a much more vulnerable position than us, so I stood up, and began trying to catch the stones, and pieces of concrete, that were being thrown at us. I succeeded in catching a few, and hurled them straight back at the Senegalese fans on the ground. It felt good to be fighting back, but I was aware that my actions would be drawing attention to me, and when Adama pulled on my arm, and begged me to get back behind the wall, I took her advice, and sat back down in relative safety.

I was really glad I had, because the next development was that I thought I heard the sound of gunfire, coming from inside the stadium. I don't know if the soldiers were using live rounds or not, but the sound of gunfire concentrated my mind wonderfully, and I asked Adama, and Solomon, if they were ready to make a move. I decided that our best course of action was to get back to the car as quickly as possible, and then try and make our way back to The Gambia, as soon as we could.

By now Farmara had reappeared, and he was spoiling for a fight. He said that he would take his chances, and try and get a lift back on one of the coaches, with some of the other Gambian fans, so we left him to it, and gingerly made our way towards the exit.

When we got outside the ground, the three of us started to make our way across the car park, in the direction of the car. There were people milling around all over the place, and then the Senegalese troops started firing tear gas into the middle of us. I told Adama to follow me, and not to hesitate, and we coughed, and stumbled, our way across the car park. Solomon was still with us as we reached the road, and we quickly made our way to where we had left the car.

I was very relieved to see that it was still in one piece, and the fact that it was a Peugeot probably helped. Senegal is a former French colony, and Peugeot is, of course, a French make of car, and this fact had probably saved it from being smashed up in the middle of what had become a full-scale riot. We jumped into the car, and started driving through the chaos that was all around us. We soon cleared the danger area, and after consulting with Adama, and Solomon, I decided to go back to The Gambia the quick way, through the border, at a place called Barra.

We made it out of Dakar without any problems, but by now the news of what had happened at the match had spread like wildfire through all the Senegalese towns, and villages, on our route, and as we approached the first village on our journey, I could see that all was not well. I had tucked in behind a coach that was carrying Gambian fans back from the match, and as we drove through the middle of the village, we were suddenly bombarded with stones, and lumps of wood, from both sides of the road. I got even tighter to the coach in front of me, and it absorbed most of the assault, so the Peugeot was relatively unscathed, but the coach had sustained some serious damage. Its front windscreen was smashed to pieces, and most of the side windows had gone as well. The Gambian fans inside the coach seemed to have come through relatively unscathed, and we carried on in our tiny makeshift convoy of two.

This ordeal was repeated in almost all the towns, and villages we drove through, on the way to the border, and by the time we finally neared The Gambia, I was exhausted, and not a little angry. The car was beginning to make some really unpleasant noises, and as we drew up at the border, I was very relieved to stop driving.

At the border things took a turn for the worse. I pulled up at a makeshift roadblock, to be surrounded on all sides by youths armed with knives, machetes, and wooden clubs. One of the youths approached the front of the car, and put a hammer through the car's windscreen. Another came up to my window, and started screaming at me, demanding to know if we were Senegalese. I had had just about enough by now, and I reached into the door- well, for the piece of lead piping, that I always carried with me in the car. The guy at the window must have read my intentions, because he started saying, "do you want to know me?" while waving his machete in my face. I looked over to Adama, who was sitting in the passenger seat, and saw that one of the youths had a pair of scissors, that were aimed directly at her head. Discretion immediately seemed the better part of valour, so I put the lead piping back in its place, and sat back down in my seat.

By now I had sussed out that the boys were Gambians, who had heard what had happened at the match, and were now looking for revenge, so I figured that once we had explained who we were, it would probably be all right. Adama had realised this as well, and she laid into them verbally with all her might. "We are Gambians just like you," she shouted, and then she added, "do you know what we have just passed through? You should be ashamed." Adama's display of righteous indignation seemed to take the wind out of their sails, like it always did when she tongue- lashed her fellow Africans, and they quickly calmed down, apologised to us, and then waved us through to the ferry port.

By now we were beginning to hear rumours of what had happened since the match had finished. One rumour had it that a Gambian police post near the border had been stormed by some Senegalese youths, and that three policemen had been shot, and killed. The Gambian youths had heard this rumour too, and it had whipped them up into a frenzy of rage, and retribution.

To get back to The Gambia, we had to go on the ferry, and where the cars had been queuing up to get on board, there was a long line of burnt out vehicles, that had been set on fire by a gang of Gambian youths, in revenge for what had happened in Dakar. On the Gambian side of the border it was even worse. The news, and rumours, had spread through The Gambia like a bush fire, and it appeared that many more Gambian youths had gone on the rampage.

The main market, in the town of Serrekunda, was nearly completely owned by Senegalese people, and some Gambian youths had set fire to a large part of it, and burned it to the ground. We also heard that large gangs of Gambian youths had been going from compound to compound, in the villages, and towns, and beating up anyone they thought to be Senegalese.

104

Through all this chaos, and mayhem, we finally managed to get across on the ferry, and when we reached the other side, and tried to drive out of the port, the car made a horrible noise, and juddered to a halt. It was clear that we wouldn't be going any further on our own steam, in the Peugeot, that day, so when I noticed a very large, well-built, Rastafarian standing at the side of the road, next to his car, I immediately negotiated a price with him for a tow back to Kololi, and we set off on the last leg of our journey.

The towing proved to be far from easy experience. The rope kept jerking between the Rastafarian's car, and the Peugeot, which meant that he kept leaning out of his window, and berating me for not keeping the rope taught. He was cursing me, and I was cursing back at him, for the whole trip, and by the time we reached our destination tempers were frayed on both sides.

I went to hand him the money, for the price that we had agreed, and he immediately demanded more, saying that he hadn't realised what a strain it would put on his car. I refused to hand over so much as another penny, and an argument broke out between us.

This was the final straw for me. I couldn't believe that after all the dangers we had faced in getting back to The Gambia, now someone was trying to rip me off for a tow. We were coming close to blows, when I let out an exasperated, "JESUS CHRIST" at the top of my voice. The Rastafarian jerked as if he had been shot, "Jesus is my name," he said, and with that, the bad feeling between us disappeared as quickly as it had arisen, and we both calmed down, and shook hands. We settled up amicably on both sides, said goodbye to Solomon, and then Adama, and I, finally got back to our little room, just before midnight, after a fraught, and dangerous, 7-hour journey.

It had been my second experience of an African football match, and it wasn't one that I was likely to forget in a hurry. It was amazing to see how these mainly calm, and gentle, people could be ignited to such extremes of violence so quickly. It occurred to me that this part of Africa was a powder keg, just waiting for a spark to ignite it. The West African people have to put up with so much on a daily basis, that when they blow, they really blow. It was clear to me that if things kicked off in this part of the world, the best thing you could do would be to head for the hills as quickly as possible, and not look back till you were safely out of harm's way.

I didn't blame the Gambian, and Senegalese people, for reacting like this occasionally, it was quite understandable given the circumstances. When I thought of some of the terrible things that had happened in this part of the world, in places like Sierra Leone, Liberia, and the Cote D'Ivoire, I prayed that an unfortunate set of circumstances wouldn't precipitate the same kind of carnage to occur one day, in Senegal, and The Gambia.

Chapter 9 – A New Life

I soon settled back into my daily routine, with egg sandwiches for breakfast, in our little room, in the compound in Kololi, and then days spent on the beach, shooting the breeze with my fishermen friends, playing games of barefoot football, and going for long swims, out to sea, on my own. It was an idyllic lifestyle, and the days rolled nicely into one another. It was amusing to see the newly arrived tourists run out of their hotels, and on to the beach as soon as they could. They looked incredibly white, and flabby, and they seemed slightly deranged, as they ran shouting, and screaming, down to the sea. My mind and body were now nicely tuned in to the African way of life, and seeing these people, with their rampant egos, and childlike behaviour, made me feel that I was now living on a different planet to them, let alone a different continent. It wasn't that I felt superior to them, it was just that the way they were acting seemed so totally inappropriate to where they were, that, if anything, I just felt completely removed from them, and their way of life.

The more adventurous souls among them would sidle up next to us, and make tentative enquiries about going on a fishing trip. I did my best to help persuade them that it was a worthwhile thing to do, but this was about as far as my interaction with them went. When we got a trip, the boys would often let me come along for a token sum, and I would do my best to buy lunch for us all when we got back. It felt really good to be so accepted by my new friends, and I felt far more comfortable with them than, with the spoiled tourists, who I was occasionally forced to mix with. All the boys on the beach were really happy that I had married a "sister", and when I took Adama down to meet them one day, they all agreed that Adama was a good "sister," and not with me purely for financial gain. I knew this anyway, but it was nice to have their tacit approval on the matter, and I was really pleased that they liked, and respected, Adama.

On the way down to the beach in the mornings, I would have to walk past a group of taxi drivers, sitting under a tree. One of them must have seen me with Adama one day, for as I walked past he shouted after me, "she is only with you because you are a white!" I didn't bite, and I was really glad I knew Adama as well as I did, so his words bounced harmlessly off me. Dealing with resentment was a daily thing for me in The Gambia, and if I'm honest sometimes it really got to me. Most of the time though I was so happy, and fulfilled, that I just accepted it as part of day to day life for me while I was there, and I tried not to react if I could help it. It was completely understandable, given the disparity of my situation compared to nearly everyone around me, so I tried not to take it to heart.

I could, however, be caught off guard, and one night when I was walking home, a Gambian youth cheekily said to me, "goodnight Toubab." I was tired, and fractious, after a long day down at the beach, and I responded with a tirade of abuse. It took me a while to calm down, and when I did, I reflected that it was all very well trying to be like St. Francis of Assisi, but I had to remember that I was human too, and there would be times when I got things badly wrong in my interactions with the locals.

The Gambian lad had the last laugh though, for the next morning, when I was walking to the beach, a car went past with him in the back, with some of his mates. They spotted me, and they all shouted out "Toubab", in unison, at the top of their voices. I could hear them laughing as they drove away, and although I felt a bit annoyed, and rather embarrassed, I couldn't help feeling that I

108

had got what I deserved, for my completely over the top reaction, the previous night.

One day I was walking home, on my usual route, which took me along the beach, as far as the Leybato Beach Bar, and then up behind it to the main road back to Kololi. As I was passing by a block of luxury apartments, I noticed a diminutive Vietnamese looking man, standing outside them. I greeted him, and continued on, and he suddenly called out to me. "What are you doing here in The Gambia"? As I wasn't really sure myself what I was doing there, I decided to tell him I was a writer, on a bit of a sabbatical. "Have I got a story for you" he said, and he beckoned me inside the apartment block. It turned out that the man's name was Minh To, and that he owned the apartment block we were now sitting in. After offering me a cup of tea, he proceeded to tell me the most amazing story of survival, and success, that I had ever heard.

Minh-To had been a soldier, in the North Vietnamese army, in the latter stages of the Vietnam war, between the North of the country, and the United States backed South Vietnamese government. He had been blown- up, shot, seen his friends killed in front of him, and had somehow survived to tell the tale. He told me that his girlfriend had been murdered in front of him, by American soldiers, and there was no doubting the authenticity, and veracity, of his story. He had a pathological hatred of Americans, and said that he could never forgive them for what they had put him through.

After the war, Minh had somehow got himself to Hong Kong, and had then come over to the UK, in the early 1970's, as part of the influx of what was then called, "The Boat People". Once in the UK, he settled in Manchester, and began selling clothes out of the back of a van. Over the next ten years his business grew to include owning supermarkets, and various other businesses, and by the

109

time I met him he was a bona fide multi-millionaire, who had decided to settle in The Gambia for a while.

It was a truly astonishing story, and when he had finished speaking, he asked me if I wanted to write his autobiography. Not wanting to turn down such an opportunity, I agreed that I would, and I promised that I would contact him when I had to eventually return to the UK.

There was an unmistakable air of menace about Minh-To, and I wondered what I was potentially getting into, but like everything else on this trip, meeting Minh –To seemed to have happened for a reason, and I decided not to worry about it, and try and deal with it when I returned to England.

Soon after meeting Minh-To, I decided to go to Banjul, to have a look around The Gambia's capital city. Apart from the market, there was not a lot there, apart from a few eateries, and some buildings that looked like they housed offices of some sort. It was nothing like the European capital cities that I had visited, and even bore little resemblance to Dakar, but it seemed lively enough, and I ventured out into its dusty streets.

The Standard Charter bank had its main branch in Banjul, and I took some money out to do a little shopping. I wandered down the main street, and suddenly became aware of being tracked by a young girl. It was the girl that I'd bought a plate of chips for, in a restaurant in Senegambia, when I'd first arrived in The Gambia, and she came up to me, and tagged along by my side.

She couldn't have been more than fifteen years old, and I felt slightly uncomfortable, as she began holding on to my arm, in a rather over-friendly way, and making it plain at how delighted she was to see me. My sense of unease increased dramatically, when she spotted a stall selling underwear, pulled me towards it, and began selecting various articles of skimpy lingerie, and asking me if she would look good in them.

I didn't know where to put myself, but I eventually managed to get her away from the stall, and, not wanting to be unkind, said that I would drop her off back in Serrekunda, where she lived. The drive back was fairly uneventful, but when I pulled over to let her out, she started to demand money from me. I wouldn't give her any, and when she started to make a scene I hastily got her out of the car, and drove off.

A couple of weeks later I was in Banjul, with Adama, and a middle-aged woman saw me, and began haranguing me in Woolof. I couldn't understand what she was going on about, and then it suddenly dawned on me that she must have seen me with the girl, and thought that I was some kind of depraved sex tourist. Adama must have understood what she was saying, but she pulled me away, saying that the woman must be mad. She never quizzed me about it, and I hoped she knew me well enough to know that there was no substance to what the woman had been saying.

It was now the beginning of July, and it was getting stiflingly hot. As the long, hot, dry season was nearing its end, it seemed as if the land itself was audibly crying out for some relief. The red soil was baking in the streets, and the land was as dry as a desert. All the trees, and bushes, were parched, and brown, and everyone seemed to be carrying an extra 50 pounds on their backs, as they trudged through the village, on their way to whatever daily chores they had to attend to.

Even the children, who were normally so boisterous, seemed to be flagging, as they listlessly kicked their footballs around, in the middle of the dusty streets of Kololi. Being a comparatively rich

111

"Toubab", it wasn't so bad for me. I would still spend each day down at the beachside, where the sea breeze gave some relief from the unrelenting hot weather, and I had plenty of money for food, and cool drinks, whenever I needed them.

On one of these mornings, when I was preparing to leave our little room, my mobile phone rang, and it was Adama on the other end of the line. She had left earlier that morning to go to work, but unbeknownst to me had instead gone to visit the doctor. "Are you sitting down Mr Coughlin"? She asked. I said that I was, and the next words she said to me completely stunned me. "You are going to be a father, I'm having a baby", she said. "Are you sure", I said, "are you absolutely sure"? "Yes Mr Coughlin", (Adama always referred to me like this) "I am as sure as I can be, the doctor has done a test, and he tells me that I have a child inside me". I sat down, this was wonderful news. "I'm so happy", I told her, "do you know when it's due"? "The doctor tells me that I am eight weeks pregnant", said Adama, and after some quick mental calculations I worked out that it would be due around February time. "Don't worry about a thing", I told her, "we are going to be a family".

It's a strange thing to say, but I was happy that I was happy. It must have been reassuring for Adama too. I only had to look at Maryama, and Diego, two doors down to know that being left with a child after a fling with a "Toubab" was a pretty common occurrence in this part of the world, and I was determined that I was going to do all I could to do the right thing by Adama. It wasn't a very hard decision to make, because I truly loved her, and all I could see were happy times ahead for us all.

Now that Adama was pregnant, I started scheming about how, when the time came, I was going to get us all back to the UK. Residency visas are notoriously hard to get for Great Britain, and

112

West Africa is a part of the world very suspiciously viewed by the authorities. Added to this was the fact that I had no visible means of support in the UK, so it seemed to me that we were faced with a very tricky problem indeed. I still had a kind of incurable optimism though, and I made up my mind that come hell or high water, our family was going to stay together, whatever it required me to do.

As the rainy season approached, it got hotter and hotter, until one day, in the middle of July, the clouds burst, and the rains came. I was in our little room, getting ready to go to the beach, when it started raining, and Adama had already set off for work at The Senegambia Beach Hotel. I gradually became aware that Haddy had come out of her room, and was now singing, in the rain, outside in the yard. I opened the door, looked out, and saw her dancing in the rain, with just a pair of knickers on. The sight excited me, and she carried on dancing, until she looked up, and saw me standing in the doorway, with my eyes fastened on her. It must have been obvious what was going through my mind, because as soon as she saw me, she stopped dancing, and retreated back inside her room. It had been an uncomfortable moment for both of us, and I was glad that Haddy had nipped it in the bud, by going back into her room. I still had a lot of western traits about me, and the sight of Haddy, in her underwear, had aroused, and excited me.

In the west, we are constantly being bombarded with images of scantily clad women, and we are almost conditioned to be excited by the sight of naked flesh. In The Gambia people tended to have a much healthier attitude towards sex, and nudity, unfettered as they were by western advertising, and commercial manipulation. I had reacted to the sight of Haddy dancing in her underwear, in a way that was totally predictable, given my culture, and upbringing.

113

I still had a long way to go before I successfully bridged the gap between two so completely different cultures, and ways of life, and it was another reminder to me of how important it was to control myself, while I was living in my adopted country.

Now that the rains had come, life changed for us all. Most mornings the passageway outside our little hut had to be swept clear of the six, or seven, inches of water that had been deposited by the previous night's storms, and every day would find either Adama, or myself, brushing away the previous night's rain, from outside our front door. It was muggy, and humid, nearly all the time, and even on the beach it was hard to get any relief from the relentless heat.

I don't know how the people in the crowded towns like Serrekunda, and Brikama, managed to survive at all, where there wasn't even the faintest breeze to alleviate the sauna-like atmosphere, and it must have been akin to living in a sweat lodge for them, during the summer months. The rains brought large pools of stagnant water, which bred mosquitoes, which in turn brought widespread malaria to a lot of the population. I had abandoned my antimalarials after my adverse reaction to sunlight, so I took my chances, along with everybody else.

Adama had started to get quite sick now. The pregnancy was taking its toll on her, and the conditions, and the fact that she was a poor eater, contributed to making her very unwell. We decided that it might be best if she went to her mum's compound in Sifoe for a little bit, so that she could rest, and be looked after, so I took her down there in the car one morning, and returned to Kololi.

When I got back inside our little room, without Adama being there, it suddenly felt so wrong. I immediately realised just what a rock she had been for me, during my time in The Gambia, and I also knew that it was getting near to the time when I would have to return to the UK.

I was running out of money, and the tenant that was in my flat in King's Cross, was due to leave. The thought of going back was not a happy one. I was going to have to go back to the mess I had left behind when my mum died. I had run away from debts, unhappiness, and sorrow, and I had found a brief respite from all those things here in The Gambia. The problem was that it was an unsustainable situation, and there was no alternative, but to go back and face the music.

I sold the car for pretty much the same price I had paid for it in the UK, and decided to spend my last two weeks in The Gambia, down in Kartong, at the Boboi Beach Motel, so I could be near to Adama, who was now in the hospital, at Gunjur. She had contracted malaria, and the complications with her pregnancy, combined with that, had made her extremely ill. This had resulted in her family placing her in the hospital, where they hoped that she would be better looked after.

It was horrible to see her in there, so ill, while knowing all the time that I would soon have to leave her. I did my best to reassure her that I wasn't just going to vanish from her life, but there wasn't much more I could do, so I settled down at Boboi Beach, and spent the next two weeks swimming, reading endless books, and making periodic visits to see Adama in the hospital. I couldn't spend all my time with her, because the heat inland was just too much for me to bear, and I was frightened of getting sick as well. I needed to stay healthy if I was to have any chance of returning to The Gambia, and taking care of my soon to be, young family, so I made the decision to spend the majority of my time close by, but in the relatively healthy environment of the Boboi Beach Motel.

The last thing I had to do was to say goodbye properly to my mum. Just before I left Boboi Beach for the last time, I took a pen and paper, and wrote a eulogy for her. I wrote about her life, and the kind of person she had been, and I took the letter, and sealed it in a bottle. I then swam about half a mile out to sea, and threw the bottle into the water. As I threw the bottle, I hoped that one day someone would find it, and read about what a terrific person she had been, and that in some small way it would help to keep her memory alive, in the universal consciousness of the planet.

I was also trying to find some kind of closure for myself, and I wanted to say goodbye to her in my own way, as I had felt unable to attend her funeral back in the UK.

The day before my flight, I returned for one final night, in our little room in Kololi. I gave some of my stuff away to various people, and visited the beach to say goodbye to my friends among the fishermen. I was trying to stay positive, but I was feeling very sad. I knew how ill Adama was, and I didn't relish the thought of being parted from her. She was so ill, that I feared for her, and our unborn child's lives, and I didn't know if either of them was going to survive while I was back in the UK.

On the morning of my departure, I got a huge surprise. Adama had somehow raised herself from her sickbed, and had come up from Sifoe, to say goodbye. I could tell that it had taken everything she had to make this gesture, and it strengthened my resolve to do the right thing by her, and my unborn child. I told her not to worry, and urged her to have faith in me. I told her that I would be back in time for the birth of our child, and that somehow or other I would sort everything out.

I left Adama, and The Gambia, and flew back to England, on 29th Aug 2003. It was the start of a difficult time for me, but one in

116

which I was determined that I would do everything I could to make sure that I was back in time for the birth of our son, the following February.

Chapter 10 – Back to Reality

I arrived in England, and went straight back to my little flat in Kings Cross. The culture shock that I experienced was tremendous. I felt like a stranger in my own country, and the hotchpotch of all the different nationalities in central London, staggered, and bemused me. I spent the first two days, lying on my bed, gazing up at the ceiling fan as it whirred overhead, mirroring the steady whirring of my brain, as I tried to work out what I needed to do. I hadn't told anyone that Adama was pregnant, so I decided to go and visit my Dad, and tell him the news.

I travelled up to Nottingham, sat him down, and told him that he was going to be a Granddad. The first words that came out of his mouth were, "what a mess". Hold on a minute, I thought, this isn't going to plan. I had expected him to be delighted, and supportive, but my Dad, ever the realist, had immediately seen the ramifications of my statement, and had just come out with his first thought.

On reflection I could see what he meant. I was back in England, penniless, with no job, and with a young, pregnant wife, 3500 miles away, in a third world country. On the face of it the situation didn't look too bright, but I was determined to be optimistic though, and I did my best to assuage his fears for me. I knew what I had to do, but I really didn't know if I would be strong enough to do it.

I returned to London, and started scouring the papers for a suitable job. I applied for a job as a chauffeur, went for an interview in a posh London hotel, and was delighted when I was informed that the position was mine.

The night before I was due to start work, I had what can only be described as a crisis of confidence. The depression that had intermittently plagued me since my early twenties, had returned with a vengeance, and I knew that I wasn't going to turn up for work in the morning. The returning depression was threatening my sobriety, and the only realistic course of action open to me was to swallow my pride, and try and focus all my energies on staying sober.

Instead of turning up for my first day at work, I went to one of my old support groups in the Pentonville Road. As I started sharing what was going on for me I realised that I was in trouble. I was missing Adama sorely, and I was worried sick about how I was going to straighten the whole situation out. For the next five months, I went to one support group after another to maintain my sobriety. I was speaking to Adama every day on my house phone, and I soon ran up an unmanageable debt of over £500 to British Telecom. I was sending Adama money from time to time, and to economise, I started eating at soup kitchens, with someone I had met at one of the meetings I was going to. It was a hard, and worrying time, but I kept telling myself that however tough I thought it was for me, Adama had it tougher.

About the time the baby was due, I swallowed my pride again, and asked my Dad if he would let me have some money, so I could go back for the birth of my child. My Dad's bark can be a lot worse than his bite at times, and he readily agreed to help me. I'll say this for my Dad he can seem really harsh, and tough, and in a lot of respects he personifies these characteristics, but he has a heart of gold, and he was only too willing to help me do the right thing, and go back to be with Adama and my unborn child.

Before I went back to The Gambia, I had one thing that I had to do. I had promised Minh-To, the Vietnamese man that I had met,

119

that I would write his biography, and I set about trying to find a ghostwriter, who would be up to the job. I scoured the internet, and finally settled on a writer called Julie, who was a Cambridge graduate, and who had had a couple of fairly successful publications. I rang Julie, and arranged to meet her in a coffee shop in Hammersmith, to try and sell her Minh-To's story.

Julie turned out to be a lovely person, very bright, and very pleasing on the eye, and after I had given her the background on Minh-To, she seemed very keen to take the job on. I negotiated a small percentage with her, for any possible future profits, and I gave her Minh To's contact details, so she could arrange a time to fly out to The Gambia and meet him.

I flew back to The Gambia on 5th Feb 2004, and immediately got in touch with Minh-To, who had offered to put myself, and Adama, up in one of his luxury apartments for a week. He also loaned me his Mercedes for a few days to get around in, and I felt like Napoleon returning from Elba as I drove around the dusty streets again, trying to re-familiarise myself with my surroundings.

Adama was in the last few days of her pregnancy, and it was strange to see the tiny delicate woman I had first met, so swollen, and full of child. The days we spent in Minh's apartment were precious, and helpful. It gave Adama a break from the noise, and mayhem of life in the compound, and it eased me back into being in The Gambia after 6 months in the UK.

When our time at Minh's came to an end, I moved into the compound with Adama, and her sisters, Margaret, and Mary, and her niece Emmo. They were now living in a place called Mangi, which was closer to Serrekunda, but further from the beach than Kololi had been.

I had been back about 3 days, when, on awakening, Adama told me that she was going to go to the hospital, and she told me to carry on down to the beach as normal. I spent the day reacquainting myself with my friends among the fishermen, and when I got back later that evening, her sister Margaret came up to me at the gate of the compound, and said four words which stopped me in my tracks. "You have a son", she said.

I'd had no idea that Adama was going to give birth, when she told me she was going to the hospital, and I couldn't believe that she had walked by herself, to the hospital, to have our baby delivered.

I went inside the compound, and I saw Adama lying on the bed. She looked exhausted, but fiercely proud, and in her arms she had a tiny little bundle containing our son. I put my little finger out, and the baby grasped it in one of his tiny hands. It was an awe-inspiring moment. Had my whole journey been about this new life that had replaced the one that I had lost, before I first came to The Gambia? My mum was dead, but now I had a child of my own.

It really spelt out the natural order of things to me, and I knew that part of my Mum now existed in this little baby, that was lying in his mother's arms, in front of me. I made a promise at that moment that I would do everything in my power to make sure that our family stayed together.

I couldn't believe the way things had worked out for me, and it felt amazing to think that I was now responsible for my own family at last. I had lived a pretty wasted life before I went to Africa, thanks mainly to my alcoholism, and associated mental health problems, but now I had a fantastic wife, and a beautiful baby boy, and I was determined to do my best for them.

Now that the baby was born, the next thing on the agenda was that a Naming ceremony would have to be held for him. This is an important tribal tradition in this part of the world, and as Adama was a member of the Manjago tribe, the ceremony would be held with her family, in the countryside, at Sifoe.

I gave Adama 5000 dalasi (about £100) to give to her mum, so she could get the things needed for the Naming Ceremony. Out of this she bought a large pig, a goat, plenty of rice, soft drinks, and an assortment of local vegetables. I invited my fishermen friends from the beach, and Adama told members of her family to come along as well. We set a date for a week from when the baby was born, which was the traditional time to hold it, and started preparing for the upcoming party.

On the day of the ceremony, we took a bush taxi to Sifoe, and when we arrived the preparations were in full swing. The courtyard of the compound held a couple of very large cooking pots, and all of Adama's dad's wives were hard at work, stirring, and adding spices, to the contents of them. There was a delicious smell in the air, and people were arriving in twos, and threes, to join the celebration. Before the party could get in full swing, we had to have the formal ceremony.

Adama was put in a back bedroom, while an assortment of family elders came in to bless her, and the baby. As the father, it fell to me to name our son, and I decided that he should be named after both our fathers, and his name should contain the surnames of both our families. Therefore it came to pass that our son was given the auspicious title of, "Joseph, Farumose, Corea, Coughlin". Adama's family were delighted that Adama's father had been honoured in this way, and her cousin Mary came up and thanked me profusely.

I was really pleased that her family were so happy with the name, and I was sure that I had made the right decision to include Adama's dad's name, and surname, in Joe's new title. After the baby was named, I went back outside, and a few minutes later a procession of women emerged from the house, with Adama at the front, holding the baby. They were chanting, and invoking the spirits to bless the new child, and they traipsed out of the compound, and then back into the house. They repeated this formality three times, and then everybody dispersed back into the general throng.

Now the formalities were over, the party could begin in earnest. Someone had set up a sound system, and it began blaring out the lively Senegalese music that I had begun to become quite fond of. The next thing on the agenda was to slaughter the two animals that had been bought to feed everyone. The pig and goat were despatched, both by having their throats cut, and being left to bleed to death. I had decided to video the proceedings with a camera that I had borrowed from my friend Maison's mum, and I wondered how the slaughtering of the animals would be received by my friends back home, when I showed them the tape.

When the animals had expired, the pig was chopped up, and put in the cooking pots, while the goat was skinned, and left hanging by his neck from a tree, to dry in the sun. When the food was finally ready it proved to be well worth the wait. The women had made two massive portions of benechin, one of pork, and the other of mutton, and they were both absolutely delicious.

Most of my friends from the beach had turned up, and although they were generally quite shy, and reserved, I could see that they were enjoying the feast. Some people had brought some beer along, and it wasn't long before a drunken fight broke out between two of Adama's male relatives. The two men were separated, and I

123

took one of them for a long walk into the surrounding countryside to calm him down. Having always been a bit of a hothead myself I could understand how he was feeling, and it was very gratifying to be the peacemaker, instead of the person that was causing the trouble. Once the guy had calmed down, we went back to the party, and he made up with his protagonist.

Gambian people generally don't hold on to grudges, and soon the two of them were laughing, and dancing around together again, like nothing had happened. We spent the afternoon eating, drinking, chatting, and dancing, and as the evening drew on people began to leave in dribs and drabs. By about ten o' clock there was only close family left at the party, and the proceedings gradually came to an end.

It had been a good day. Joe had his name, Adama's family were happy that their name had been included in the ceremony, and the little bit of trouble that had threatened to mar proceedings had been dealt with quickly, and with very little bloodshed.

My cultural transformation was now almost complete. I felt infinitely more at home with my Gambian family than I did with the friends that I had left behind in the UK. I felt that I had more in common with the Gambians than I had with my own people. I had maintained a daily struggle to remain sober, and they had to endure a daily struggle just to stay alive. It felt that my path perfectly matched up with theirs at that point in my life, and now I had a son, who had been born in The Gambia, to cement my bond with them.

I would never have been able to foresee this when I stopped drinking six years previously, and it seemed that I now really was "living the life beyond my wildest dreams", that had been promised to me when I first got sober, all those years before, in

London. I stayed in The Gambia for two more weeks after the naming ceremony, and when the time came to leave it was an awful wrench.

It had been hard enough when it was just Adama that I was leaving, but now I had to leave behind my baby boy as well. I had no idea how I was going to deal with the practicalities of living in the UK, without a job, while trying to maintain a wife, and baby, living in one of the world's poorest countries, almost 3500 miles away. I suppose that I had been totally irresponsible getting married, and starting a family, before I even had a regular job, but the connection with Adama had been so meaningful, and natural, that when I was with her everything just seemed so straightforward. The problems always began for me when I was left on my own for too long, back in the UK, and I was due for another spell of that again now.

As I expected, when I flew back to the UK, my mental health immediately took a turn for the worse. I became chronically depressed, and anxious, in a very short space of time, and in that frame of mind it took all my energy, and resources, just to do what I had to do, in order to stay sober. I found it impossible to look for a job, to enable me to help support my young family back in The Gambia, so I resumed eating in soup kitchens, and the little money that I saved I would send monthly to Adama, to help her to look after the baby.

I carried on like this until August, when I went to visit my brother, and his wife, at their house in Worthing. My brother and I had a silly argument about our different life philosophies, and all my worry, anger, and resentment, boiled up in me, and I stormed out of his house before I said, or did, something that I would have regretted for the rest of my life.

My situation was dire now. I was hanging on to my sobriety by the skin of my teeth, and I didn't know how long I would be able to keep it up. In desperation, I turned once again to my dad for help. I asked him if he would give me £10000 so I could return to The Gambia, to be with my family, and start a little fishing business on the beach. To my utter astonishment my dad immediately said yes, and his only concern was why I hadn't asked him sooner. It was a huge relief to suddenly have a solution to my problems, and I quickly started making preparations for a return to my family in The Gambia.

This time, when I left England, it had an air of permanence about it. I had a little party for my sober friends in my support groups, and one of them, an ex-captain in the Parachute regiment called John, came with me, and my dad, to the airport to see me off. John seemed genuinely in awe of the adventure that I was about to embark on, and I felt flattered that someone who spent his spare time base jumping from empty office blocks, in the city, on Sunday mornings, looked on me with obvious envy, and amazement.

Before I left, I dipped into the £10,000 to buy some various things that I thought I would need when I was back in The Gambia. Among the things I bought were a decent pair of open-toed sandals, a pair of binoculars, a car stereo, and a portable CD player. I bought a few things for Adama too, including some nice perfume, and a few clothes that I thought she would like to wear. I assembled everything that I thought I would need, spent my last night in King's Cross, and left at 6am, on a Wednesday morning, for the airport, with my dad, and John, accompanying me in the car.

When the plane took off from Gatwick, at the end of August 2004, I didn't know when, if ever, I would be coming back to

126

Britain. I wasn't worried, because as far as I was concerned, my family, and my life, were now in The Gambia, and I was going to give it my best shot to try and make things work out. To be honest, at the time, there weren't a lot of alternatives open to me.

The first emotion I felt when I stepped into the airport terminal in The Gambia was disappointment. I had been expecting Adama to be waiting for me when the plane touched down, but when I scoured the sea of faces waiting for the new arrivals, Adama was not among them. I swallowed my disappointment, purchased a coke at the small bar in the airport, and settled down to wait for her. The minutes ticked by, and there was still no sign of Adama. I got another coke, and waited some more. After about half an hour I saw a group of people coming through the airport doors. It was Adama, cradling Joseph in her arms, and a Gambian youth who I assumed that she had got to bring her to the airport.

In the U.K we work on Greenwich Mean Time, but in The Gambia something jokingly called Gambian Maybe Time is employed, and I had forgotten this during my short spell back in England. By Gambian standards Adama wasn't really late at all, and after a family hug we jumped in the back of the waiting car, and headed back to the compound in Mangi.

It was such a relief to be reunited with my family, and when we arrived back at the house it was great to see that Adama's sister Margaret was still living with us. Margaret was a truly lovely person. She was a lot fuller figured than Adama, possessed of a lovely nature, and never seemed to let things get her down. She seemed to be permanently cheerful, and her presence brightened up the house no end. I couldn't have married into a nicer family, and I knew how lucky I had been in meeting Adama, and not someone who was purely interested in me because I was white, and possibly well off, which I patently was not.

127

Now that I was back I set about getting things organised. The first thing I had to do was to organise some transport. I knew a boy called Tamba, who hung out down at the Senegambia strip, running a small taxi business, so I went to see him to see if he knew of any cars for sale. It turned out that he had a little Suzuki jeep that he wanted to get rid of, so I took my mechanic, Omar, who had worked on the Peugeot, to check it out. After giving it the once-over, Omar gave it the thumbs up, so I bought it for 50,000 Dalasi, (about £1,000) and ticked it off my list.

Once I had the car, I set about looking for a boat. There was an Englishman called Mark, who had been living in The Gambia for about 15 years with his wife. Between them, they ran a very successful charter fishing business, from a place called Denton Bridge, which was on the road to Banjul. I went to visit Mark, and he told me that he had an old boat that he might be willing to sell me. It was a well-used 17ft Orkney fishing boat, and as soon as I saw it I knew that it would be perfect for what I had in mind. Mark could see that I didn't pose any kind of a threat to his business, so the deal was done, and I had my very own fishing boat for the princely sum of 25,000 Dalasi (about £500).

Now I had the boat, I had to equip it, and find a crew. Finding a crew was relatively easy. I asked my friend James if he would like to be captain, and Abu, Ibu, and Solomon, made up the rest of the ship's company. I bought second-hand rods, and reels, from a small stall at Denton Bridge, lifejackets for the tourists from a shop on the Banjul highway, and nets, and gaffs, for landing the bigger fish, from the small fishing village that was located just on the outskirts of Banjul.

The last thing I got was the engine. I finally settled on a second-hand 15hp Yamaha motor, that had seen better days, but appeared to run smoothly, and once I had convinced a very sceptical James that the engine was o.k., my preparations were complete, and I was ready to start trading on the beach.

The day I brought the boat to the beach was a big event. Everyone was really excited, and I was probably the most excited of them all. There was one surreal moment when I was sitting at the Kunte-Kinte beach bar, eating a prawn cocktail, with the boat anchored a little way off-shore in front of me. People in AA speak about a sober life being "beyond their wildest dreams", and I had often wondered what they meant, but sitting there, at that moment, eating my prawn cocktail, sitting under a sun lounger, on a tropical beach, and looking at my boat decked out, and ready for action, I thought that I finally understood what they had been talking about.

Business was still relatively slow at this time of year, as it was still in the rainy season, and many tourists preferred to wait until the cooler drier weather that began in the middle of October before they visited, but we still got our first customer, and the business was up and running. The deal that I gave James for captaining the boat was ridiculously generous, and in a business sense I had pretty much cut my own throat before I had even begun. At the time though I had visions of building a successful cottage industry on the beach, and my wild optimism, and unrealistic business forecasts, were driving me on blindly.

Getting the boat ready, and putting it out to sea when we got a customer, took a bit of organising. Firstly one of the boys would be dispatched to the fish market at Bakau to get the bait for the trip. The bait that we used was large prawns that had been caught in the fishing nets off the coast of Banjul. These prawns were enormous, and it was hard to believe that they were being used as mere bait, when the same prawns would sell for a fortune in the supermarkets back in the U.K.

The next thing was that the engine had to be carried down from the small shed that it was kept in, at the side of Bibi's market. The engine was quite heavy, and although I could just about manage to bring it down to the boat, I normally left this job to either Abu, or Ibu, to take care of. The engine would be screwed on to the back of the boat, and one of the lads would be sent off to get the petrol for the trip from one of the local petrol stations. All the gear would then be loaded into the boat, and between us we would pull it down on its trailer into the sea.

The tourists that were going on the trip would be invited to get into the boat, and we would all take up our positions to try and ensure a safe launch. Abu and Ibu would stay at the front of the boat, to steady it against the incoming waves, myself, and somebody else, would take up position on either side, and Solomon would be at the back steadying the stern, while James sat in the back of the boat ready to start the engine.

Launching the boat was all about timing. James would count the waves, and when the time was right we would push the boat out into deeper water, and he would start the engine, and power off into the oncoming surf. Sometimes the front of the boat would take a big hit from one of the incoming waves, and the tourists, and the boat, would be temporarily swamped with water. This quite often caused a fair amount of panic among the paying customers, but James's calm assurance, and beaming smile, normally reassured them sufficiently to stop them diving over the side, while the rest of us held our breath, and thanked our lucky stars, that the boat was still the right way up.

The really tricky bit was bringing the boat back in after a day's fishing. The timing would have to be spot on, or the boat could be caught from behind, and turned by a large wave, leaving it side on to the sea, and prone to being capsized. Most of the time James had this procedure off to an art form, but he did occasionally get it wrong, and when he did it led to some very hairy moments for us all.

When the boat was coming in, those of us who were left on the shore would wait in the shallows to catch, and steady it, as it hurtled towards us in its bid to outrun the surf. On one occasion an overeager Gambian youth jumped in the water to try and help, and managed to get under my feet as I was trying to help bring the boat into shore. I tripped over him, and nearly went under the boat. He was only trying to help, but it was too dangerous to let people get in the way, so I got quite angry with him, and told him to mind his own business in the future.

I hadn't wanted to be unkind, but I couldn't afford to stand on ceremony down there on the beach. Although it may have been a place for relaxation, and pampering, for the tourists, it was a tough working environment for me, and I had to be as tough as everybody else down there if I wanted to survive.

Generally speaking there were always a couple of fatalities every year among the crews, and tourists, who used the small fishing boats like mine, that plied their trade off the main beach, during the high season. As I was unlicensed, and unofficial, it did cross my mind that if there was an accident involving my boat I would most likely be thrown in jail, but I couldn't be bothered worrying about it too much, and like most things at the time I just trusted to luck that it wouldn't happen to me.

Towards the end of October we came into the Barracuda season. Fishing for Barracuda was great fun. You took the boat out to where the fish were generally to be found, and then set it at a steady speed, trailing a line, with a lure attached to it. When a fish was hooked it was an exhilarating moment. Barracudas fight pretty

131

hard, and it generally took fifteen or twenty minutes to get them out of the water.

One day we caught seven big fish, which we sold to local restaurants, before splitting the money that we got for them between us. I would often save one of the fish for myself, and I would take it home to Adama, and Margaret, in the evening to make an extra special benechin, for us all, for the next day.

When the tourist industry got into full swing, at the beginning of November, it was great fun hanging out on the beach. The boat had an endless supply of customers, and my deal with James notwithstanding, I actually began to feel like I was making a reasonable amount of money. It was nice to return to the compound at night, with my pockets stuffed full with my share of the day's takings, and after my years of penury of trying to survive on benefits in central London, I felt like I was finally achieving something out in The Gambia.

The local youths on the beach soon got to know me, and it gave me a good feeling when they called out "Yo fisherman" as I walked past them, on my way to the boat, in the mornings. I began to feel my body changing again as I adapted to the incredibly healthy lifestyle, and diet, that I was enjoying, and in no time at all I felt as fit, and strong, as I had during my first eight months in The Gambia.

I decided that it was now time to christen the boat. After not much thinking at all I decided to call it "Mac's Spirit", after my mum. My mum had always hated her given name of Mildred, and as her surname was McCluskey, all her friends had called her "Mac" for short. I got a local artist to paint the name on the prow of the boat, and, for good measure, I asked him to paint a few dolphins on the side while he was at it.

Now I felt that we were properly in business, the only problem being that we didn't have the rafts of official papers, and licences that would have allowed us to operate legally off the beach. I thought about trying to legalise things many times, but the prospect of having to deal with the complicated bureaucracy that would no doubt ensue from such a course of action, put me off pursuing that idea. Besides, I kind of liked the extra dimension of risk that running the boat illegally lent to the whole operation, so I just let it slide, and carried on trying to fly under the official radar.

One day we were coming back from a fishing trip when I noticed something unusual in the water. We pulled up next to it, and I saw that it was a pelican. It looked nearly dead, so I got James to pull it into the boat, and we carried on towards the shore. When we reached land we dragged the pelican onto the beach, and I decided that I wanted to know what pelican tasted like. By this time a large group of tourists had gathered around us, and there was total outrage when I told one of the boys to finish it off. I had completely lost all European sentiments by now, and all I was thinking about was whether it would make a tasty benechin for the evening meal.

Looking back now I wish I had tried to nurse it back to health, but at the time all the pelican represented to me was an opportunity for a change in my daily diet, so I ignored the outraged tourists, and once the pelican was dispatched I took it home for Adama, and Margaret, to prepare for the evening meal. I readied myself for a tasty dinner, but when the pelican was plucked, and stripped of excess flesh, there was hardly any of it left that was edible, and the meal when it came was a poor reflection of the magnificent creature it had once been.

Chapter 11 – Visitors, Ex-pats, and Trouble in Paradise

After I had been back in The Gambia for about 6 months, my Dad made a decision to come out and visit us. I had been keeping in touch with him regularly by phone, and I was delighted that he would soon be able to see his grandson. The day he arrived I went down to the hotel to meet him, and decided that on the way back to our house I would take him for a drive through Serrekunda. It was dark by the time I picked him up, and when we got to Serrekunda, it must have seemed like a strange, and dangerous, place to him.

Serrekunda at night is loud, hectic, and unlit. There were people everywhere, and as I inched my way down the main road, two Gambian youths jumped in the back of the jeep, and asked me if I would take them to the end of the street. I was quite used to this sort of thing happening, but it was my Dad's first day in West Africa, and he looked distinctly alarmed as the two boys made themselves comfortable in the back of the car.

I remembered how I had felt when I first arrived in The Gambia, and I tried to reassure him that there was nothing to worry about, but the situation was so alien to him that my words of reassurance had very little effect, and he continued to look very ill at ease until the boys jumped off further down the road.

When we got to the compound Margaret had cooked a chicken Yassa for us all, but she had seriously overdone the chillies, so my dad's first experience of African food was extreme as well. The next day I met my dad at his hotel, and took him down the beach to where the boat was kept. He looked visibly moved when he saw that I had christened it "Mac's Spirit", in memory of my mum, and

134

his wife, and I introduced him to the boys who proceeded to make a great fuss of him.

There is still an inbuilt respect for elders in Gambian society, and it was one of the things that I really liked about this part of the world. The wisdom of age was recognised, and because of the economics of life in Gambian society, people looked after their parents when they got old, and didn't abandon them to their fate, as so often happens in most western societies. Because of this the boys treated my dad very well, and he entered into the spirit of things with his usual gusto.

My dad was over for two weeks, and while he was with us we took a boat trip up the river, and I took him down to see the snake man, who lived in the bush, down in Kartong. My Dad was in his early seventies, but he still wasn't averse to kicking a football around on the beach, or even attempting to climb a tree, using just a rope around his waist, when we were watching some palm wine tappers give a demonstration on one of our trips. Of course he was subjected to the same hassling as everyone else on the beach when he was on his own, but most of the time he was with myself, and the other fishermen, down on the beach, by the boat, so to a large extent he was spared the remorseless attention of the "Bumsters" most of the time.

My Dad's visit passed very quickly, and the day soon came when it was time to wave him off home to England again. Adama took the day off work, and she brought baby Joe down to the hotel with her, and the three of us saw his coach depart for the airport. I hoped he'd had a nice holiday, and I hoped that he was reassured about my situation in The Gambia. Adama had tried her best to make a good impression, and I was sure that amid all the excitement, and novelty, of his surroundings, that he had noticed what a great person she was, and how I couldn't have wished for a better wife, or mother for my little boy.

Now that I was settled again, I was beginning to notice the many ex-pats that had also made The Gambia their home. In our various ways we were all slightly mad, and it was interesting to me to observe the others as they tried, or didn't try, to integrate themselves into the Gambian culture.

There was a German lady called Nina, who drew my attention one day, as I was sitting at the Leybato beach bar, having my lunch. Nina was in her mid-forties, reasonably attractive, and wore a massive pair of Elton John like glasses. She was accompanied by a young Gambian lad, and it was obvious that they were in some kind of mutually beneficial relationship. Nina was giving forth on a heavy political subject, and her companion would occasionally chip in, and stroke her already well-developed ego, at the appropriate times. Nina would lap up the attention, and the young lad that she was with would work his way through a number of the local beers while they were sitting there.

These relationships between middle-aged foreigners, and young Gambian lads, were quite common, and to my still western eyes seemed wrong on so many levels, but my philosophy was, "live and let live", so I tried not to be too judgemental. Besides, I had done something similar in getting together with Adama, and although the age difference between us was only ten years, the principle was the same.

I had come to know a young Tyneside couple called Darren, and Natalie, since I had been back in The Gambia. Darren was an architect, who had set up a business designing, and building, holiday homes for British people, who had been coming to The Gambia regularly for years, and now wanted something more permanent to stay in on their trips back to the country. Darren was in his late twenties, seemed permanently angry, and seemed to be in a state of permanent frustration that things in The Gambia didn't work the same as they had for him in the UK. His wife Natalie was also in her late twenties, and was a constant fixture at Darren's side. Natalie pretty much went along with everything Darren said, and didn't seem to be allowed to have many opinions of her own.

Darren's anger seemed to me to be masking a deep-seated fear of the people whose country he was living in, and I found him arrogant, aggressive, and not possessed of very much insight about the place in which he was trying to re-invent himself.

I was sitting in an English bar one day, having a coca cola, when I noticed an Englishman holding court in the middle of the room. I listened in astonishment as he proceeded to deride everything about the country he was living in. According to this man, who I would later come to know as Paul, the Gambian people were all stupid, lazy, and dishonest, and he didn't have a good word to say about anything to do with The Gambia. As I listened to him, I felt myself getting angrier, and angrier. The man was a throwback to colonial times, when the majority of white Europeans considered themselves superior in every way to the people whose countries they had invaded, and I found what he was saying to be racist, bigoted, and extremely unpleasant to listen to.

I had an altogether different perspective to Paul. Having married Adama, and having seen how hard she worked, and how talented she was, and having seen how tough life was for the boys on the beach, I had an ever growing respect for the ordinary people of The Gambia. It was obvious to me that this man had no idea what he was talking about, and I found his particular brand of colonial racism so distasteful, that I quickly downed my drink, left the bar, and went in search of some better company.

Some of the ex-pats were the complete opposite of Paul. These guys had immersed themselves so deeply in the Gambian culture that they acted, and spoke, like black Africans. I was with Adama one day, in a shop in Senegambia, when I got talking to one of these fellows. He was chewing on a stick, like Africans sometimes do, to keep their teeth clean, and he kept referring to Adama as "Sister," ,which irked me a great deal, as he was about as Gambian as I was. Once upon a time he had been Dutch, but he was so far into his Gambian fantasy that I knew he would never emerge from it.

I was always aware that however long I lived in The Gambia, and however Gambian my life appeared to be, I would never fully understand what it meant to be a Gambian. After all, how can a person properly understand the true nature of a place unless they are a product of generations of passed down personal experience, and have all the spiritual, and family connections, that develop over thousands of years. The Dutchman cut a sad Walter Mitty-like figure to me, and my irritation was quickly replaced by pity that he had lost himself so completely.

Another type of ex-pat were the ones who had come to The Gambia to make money. All over the Senegambia strip were restaurants, estate agents, and shops, owned by foreigners who had once come to The Gambia for a holiday, and had returned to start reasonably lucrative businesses. These people worked hard, and kept a low profile, while they lived out their lives in the sun. Among these foreigners were lots of Lebanese.

The Gambia was full of Lebanese people who had originally fled the playgrounds of Beirut when the troubles started, and had come to The Gambia to make a new life for themselves, and their families. The Lebanese had fingers in most of the small, and medium-size businesses in The Gambia, and their presence was, for the most part, tolerated, and accepted, by the Gambian people.

Finally, there were the Senegalese, and the other West Africans, who had come to The Gambia as refugees from the fighting in places like Sierra Leone, the Cote D'Ivoire, and Liberia. These factions all had their little enclaves, and for the most part,(football matches aside), lived in relative peace, and harmony, with their Gambian hosts. All in all, it was an eclectic bunch of people that made up the population of The Gambia, and I loved the vibrancy that these outside influences brought to my day to day life.

Adama and I were now renting a small compound in Mangi, and Adama's sister Margaret would come by every day to clean the house, and look after baby Joe. After a couple of months, Adama's niece Emmo came to stay with us. Emmo was fifteen, still at school, and was very pretty, but also very, very, shy. After a while we had another visitor come to stay with us. His name was Mathew, and he was Adama's nephew from Guinea Bissau. Mathew was only 11 years old, and staying with us was obviously a big holiday for him. I felt that Mathew was destined for a life of poverty, and hardship, and I tried my best to bring a little sunshine, and freedom, into his life while he was with us

During the day, I would take him down to the beach with me to play football with the fishermen, and at night the four of us would sit around the table, in the front room, playing endless games of cards. Mathew was very competitive, and loved to win, and Adama would tease him remorselessly that he was cheating. Mathew would get very defensive, and eventually all four of us would fall about laughing as the situation descended into farce.

When Mathew finally had to go back to Guinea Bissau I felt very sad. He was a lovely little boy, and it had been nice to see him relax, and gain a little self-confidence, while he had been staying with us. I hoped that when he went back to Guinea Bissau his life would pan out better than I feared it would for him.

After Mathew left, everything was fine for a while, until one day a lot of noise started coming from an abandoned building, across the street. A group of young Gambian lads had decided to make the building their gathering place, and they would come together every night to chat, play cards, and blast out music, from a small transistor radio, that seemed to have an astonishingly loud volume. I sat, and seethed, night after night, when I got back home from my work on the beach, until one night I decided enough was enough, and stormed out of the house to confront them.

I had made the mistake of letting my anger fester away, and by the time I approached them my reaction was completely over the top. I went up to them, grabbed the radio, and immediately turned it off, while telling them that they needed to find another place to hang out.

Unbeknownst to me, a British woman of Jamaican descent was renting the house opposite ours for the season, and she was supplying the boys with ganja, and encouraging them to party every night. She came storming out of her house, and ran up towards me clutching a kitchen knife, while shouting that she was going to stab me. I grabbed her arm, and a small struggle ensued while she tried to turn the knife on me, and I tried to keep her at arm's length. The boys all surrounded me, and started jostling me, and it seemed for a moment that things were really getting out of control, so I let go of her arm, and tried to get the boys between me and the knife.

The Jamaican woman was making all the noise now. She was calling me a "blood claat", and still waving the knife around, and threatening to stab me, so I decided that discretion was the better part of valour, and retreated back to my house.

I hadn't realised what I had let us in for, until I returned from the beach the following night. The noise was worse than ever, and the group of five boys had turned into a large gang of about fifteen. It was plain to see that my ham-fisted attempts to address the noise situation had merely served to antagonise them, and that they now appeared to be hell-bent on making our lives a misery. I knew too that the Jamaican woman was behind the escalation of hostilities, and as I sat in the house listening to the booming music, I felt my anger rising, and rising. Adama counselled me against doing anything drastic, so we resolved to try and put up with it the best we could until a solution could be found.

The following morning I had just driven the jeep out of the gates of the compound, when I noticed something out of the corner of my eye. It was the Jamaican woman, and she was running up to my driver's window, holding a large kitchen knife again. I was a sitting duck, so I quickly put the car into gear, and sped off up the dusty street. As I drove away I could hear all the boys laughing, and the woman shouting her mouth off, and it pushed me over the edge. I slammed the car into reverse, and drove straight at the woman, who was still holding the knife. I was going to hit her, but at the last moment she dived out of the way, and into the bushes that surrounded her garden.

A declaration of war had now been made by both sides, and the situation deteriorated rapidly. I would leave the house every morning, cursing the boys sitting in the derelict building, and after I had gone, they would shout out loud enough for Adama to hear that they were going to rape her, and then burn the house down.

Adama would tell me this when I got home, and the stress of the situation really began to get to me, and I started to get more and more wound up.

I had made friends with an Englishman called John, and I asked him if he could help. John was in his early fifties, and had semi-retired to The Gambia after running his own very successful garage door company in the UK. John was tough, down to earth, and he didn't mess around. He was also an alcoholic, in the full throws of his illness, and I knew that asking for his help was a last resort, as there was no telling what he would do.

One night, when the music was absolutely unbearable, I called John, and asked him to come around to the house. John turned up five minutes later, in his Land Rover, with headlights, and spotlights, on full beam. He jumped out of the car, and immediately began to remonstrate with the boys.

John understood the power of being white in this part of the world, far better than I did, and he managed to sew some seeds of doubt in the boy's minds about what kind of consequences they could expect if they carried on terrorising myself, and Adama.. After a while, it seemed that the message had got through, and John jumped in his car, and went home. For about an hour it was peaceful outside, then the Jamaican woman came out, and it all started up again. There was no doubt that she was fanning the flames of the dispute, and I knew that we would get no peace until the situation was comprehensively dealt with.

The next morning, I drove down to the army barracks near to the Senegambia strip. They were just releasing the prostitutes that had been picked up the night before, and these poor women were milling around outside as I drove up. I asked one of the soldiers standing around if I could see his commanding officer, and he ushered me into a small room, where a captain in the Gambian army was seated. I explained the situation with the Jamaican woman, and the boys, and I asked him if he could help. I hinted at a possible monetary reward for a successful solution to my problem, and he clicked into action.

In no time at all, I was driving at the head of a small convoy of myself, and two army Land Rovers, full of Gambian soldiers. We pulled up outside the compound, and the soldiers piled out of their vehicles. They asked me to point out the troublemakers, and soon all the boys were rounded up, and placed in the back of the vehicles. There still remained the problem of the Jamaican woman, but once I pointed out where she lived, she was brought out as well, and taken along with the boys.

The soldiers took us all to a large building just off the coastal road, near Senegambia, and sat us in front of the army captain, who it appeared was going to hold a summary hearing on the matter. He questioned each of us in turn, and seemed prepared to sit there for as long as it took to get to the truth of the dispute. The Jamaican woman was crying, and saying that she had been coming to The Gambia for years, and had never had any trouble, but the captain was unmoved, and continued his interrogation.

We were in the room for a good couple of hours before a verdict was given. The boys were told in no uncertain terms that if they continued with their vendetta they would face serious consequences, which in their case would mean a beating, and possible imprisonment, and the Jamaican woman was warned about supplying them with drugs, and encouraging their bad behaviour. We were told that that was the end of it, and made to shake hands with each other before we left.

As an example of Gambian justice it was very impressive. The truth had been established, everybody had been warned, and nobody had been locked up or beaten. A good result all round as far as I was concerned.

The next morning all the problems with the neighbours had disappeared. The boys were as eager as I was to forgive, and forget, and as I struggled to close the compound gates, a few of them came over, and gave me a hand. It was like the previous six weeks had never happened, and it made me even more fond of the Gambian people. Imagine if that situation had arisen on a council estate in Peckham. The lads there would never have let it go, and they would have just laughed at a warning from the police. Gambian justice might be brutal at times, but there was no doubt that as a deterrent it was very effective. The threat of a beating had been enough to stop the problem in its tracks, and for my part I learned another valuable lesson in patience, tolerance, and how to behave appropriately in The Gambia.

The Jamaican woman wasn't able to modify her behaviour and she moved to a house in Brufut, which was a small fishing village about ten miles from the Senegambia strip. I was glad to see the back of her, and without her toxic influence on the boys, we all got along famously from then on.

That evening, when I came home from a day's fishing, I stopped by the boys, as they sat outside the derelict compound. The music was low, and there was an atmosphere of mutual respect. I gave them some of the day's catch, and a couple of hundred Dalasi for cigarettes, and "gunpowder" tea. This was how things worked in this part of the world. It didn't hurt me to be a bit generous from time to time, and in my drive for self- sufficiency, with my Gambian wife, I had neglected to observe the unwritten rule that demanded that the haves were expected to occasionally help the

144

have-nots. Now that I was behaving properly, so were the boys, and from that day on we commenced to live in perfect harmony with each other.

The combination of my rashness, and the inflammatory actions of the Jamaican woman, had almost had severe consequences for all concerned. I couldn't do anything about other people, but I could try and change my responses. I counted my lucky stars, and once again vowed not to repeat the same mistake.

It was around the time of my dispute with the neighbours that I had an unexpected stroke of luck. I had somehow got to know a British woman called Deborah, and when things were bad with the boys I had phoned her in desperation for some help. She had come over with a friend of hers to try and assist, and while I was talking to her I blurted out that I was in recovery, and was frightened that all the stress of the situation was going to drive me back to drink. Her friend asked me if I had ever been to a certain support group, and when I said that I had, she gave me the great news that there was, in fact, a weekly meeting of that group, right there in The Gambia.

I went to the meeting the following Friday, and who should I see when I walked in but Paul, the intolerant, racist, Englishman that had so appalled me when I had listened to him ranting about the Gambians, when I had run into him previously in a bar. After talking to him for a while, I realised that although he had quite an important job, he knew very little about the culture in which he was living, and he had absolutely no comprehension of how completely at odds he with the whole environment in which he was living, and working. I realised that not everyone living in The Gambia had thrown themselves into Gambian life quite as comprehensively as I had, and it helped explain, without excusing, their attitudes towards the Gambian people.

145

Paul was frustrated with what he perceived to be the inefficiency of his Gambian workforce, but he was making no allowances for the climate, culture, or the generally different way of doing things, that characterised this part of the world. I got the impression that he wanted things to run as smoothly at work, as perhaps they had for him in The UK, but from where I was standing that was never going to happen, and he seemed destined to be in a state of perpetual frustration, and anger, as long as he remained living, and working, in The Gambia.

The meeting was held in the British embassy and even in this most democratic of institutions average, every day, Gambians were not allowed inside the compound for the meetings. The justification for this, put forward by Paul, was that if Gambians were allowed into the meeting they would inevitably steal something from the home of the person where it was held. I knew this went against the traditions of this particular support group, but the ex-pats who made up the meeting were bamboozled into accepting this sorry state of affairs by Paul, whose loathing of the Gambians knew no bounds.

As a newcomer to the meeting I felt powerless to influence anyone, and to my eternal regret I didn't speak up against this blatant racism, but went along with it, albeit reluctantly. Nowadays I have a far better understanding of the traditions of this particular group, and how essential they are for the continued existence of the fellowship, and if put in the same position again I would be far more vocal in my disapproval of the shameful treatment of the Gambians, by people who should really have known better.

Daily life improved dramatically now that the problem with our neighbours had been solved, but Adama was in no mood to forgive, and forget. The threats that had been made against her, and Joe, were not something that she was able to let go of easily, and so we moved again to another house, within a compound, near the police station in Mangi. Our immediate neighbour was a good-natured, rather excitable, Gambian called Camara.

Camara was of average height, and build, very well- muscled, and about 50 years old. He had a reputation for being a bit of a medicine man, and there would be occasional visits to his home from some very sad looking young women, who would come to him to try and solve their spiritual problems. Camara also liked to play very loud music, but for some reason it didn't seem to bother me as much anymore. Margaret moved in with us to take care of Joe, while Adama and I were at work, and she brought her own new-born daughter Val to live with us as well.

I loved having the children in the house. Every day when I came back from the beach Joe would run up to greet me shouting "daddy, daddy, daddy, daddy", at the top of his voice. Little baby Val would normally be laid out on the settee, fast asleep, and Margaret would be cooking the evening meal for us all. It wasn't a luxurious life by any stretch of the imagination, but the feeling of homeliness, and family, more than made up the physical hardships, and for once in my life I really felt like I belonged somewhere.

Chapter 12 – Malaria, Diamonds, and drama on the beach

One day when I came back from my day's work on the beach, I felt really under the weather. As the evening wore on, I started to feel worse, and worse, and by the time Adama got home I was vomiting, and having severe attacks of diarrhoea. My body felt as if it was burning up, and my skin was sore to the touch. Adama said that I should go to the hospital, but I kept saying that I would be all right, and that it wasn't that bad.

After a while, when it wasn't getting any better, I had to concede that going to get help was probably the right thing to do, so we called a taxi, and headed for the all-night chemist in Serrekunda. By now my head was spinning, and while Adama spoke to the pharmacist, I wandered outside, fell to my knees in the middle of the street, and started being violently sick. Nobody seemed to find it strange to see a "Toubab" in this condition, and as nobody stopped to help, I can only assume that they were either too wary of getting involved in a "Toubab's" business, or that they probably thought that I was drunk.

Adama eventually came outside and found me, and took me to a private clinic just across the road from the pharmacy. A doctor examined me, and the first thing he asked me was whether I had been taking drugs. I told him that I didn't even drink alcohol, and after a short time, the doctor pronounced a diagnosis of malaria. It was decided that I would be admitted to the clinic, as being a "Toubab" it was thought, probably correctly, that I wouldn't be able to cope with making daily trips to the chemist for the injections that I would have to have for a short while to make me better.

I stayed in the hospital for two days, and had some of the most painful injections I have ever experienced. The size of the needle that was used to administer them, was something to behold, and when the nurse stuck it in my backside, the pain was immediate, and excruciating. The treatment was super effective though, and I began to feel markedly better soon after the first jab.

I left the hospital feeling very weak, and fragile, and when I got home I was immediately struck with a chronic case of diarrhoea that persisted for the next week. After nearly two and a half years in The Gambia this was the first time I had been ill, so I just tried to accept it, and used the time to catch up on some writing. The boat, I was sure, could take care of itself until I felt better.

When my strength returned, I started going down to the boat as usual, and I soon got back into the daily routine of trying to drum up some interest in fishing trips among the latest batches of tourists arriving on the beach on a daily basis. One day, as I was giving the boat a bit of a clean, I was approached by a rather tall black man with long dreadlocks. He was obviously not a tourist, but compared to James, Solomon, and Farmara, he looked rather soft to me, and he had a bit of a baby face. He told me that he too was known as "Fisherman", and he began to talk about diamonds.

He was originally from Sierra- Leone, but now lived in The Gambia, and he had an interesting little side-line going on. He told me that he periodically made trips by bush taxi to Sierra-Leone, for the sole purpose of purchasing conflict diamonds from the ex-rebels who lived there. He asked me if I would be interested in taking some of these diamonds from him on a sale or return basis, and he proposed that the next time I flew back to England I should take some of them with me, try and sell them, and then wire him his share of the money.

The fact that they were conflict diamonds didn't worry me at the time, as I didn't really consider the implications of this fact, and it seemed like an ideal opportunity to make a considerable amount of money with no investment up-front. I told him that I would think about it, and when he left I went over to James, and the boys, and asked them what they thought.

James warned me off this "Fisherman", telling me that he was a bad man, and a dangerous one too. All of my other friends agreed with James, and it struck me that for them to warn me about one of their peers was very unusual.

Generally James and the others trod a fine line between watching their fellow Gambians extract as much money as possible from the tourists, and trying to safeguard their white friends from getting too burned by the various hustlers down on the beach. It was a tricky situation for them a lot of the time, with divided loyalties, and potentially fierce resentment being the consequence of how they handled this delicate state of affairs that was played out a hundred times a day, down on the sand. For James to have outright warned me off this "Fisherman" was very unusual, but I didn't take much notice, and figured I'd play along for the time being, and see where it ended up.

I continued to allow myself to be groomed by "Fisherman", and one day when I was at "Leybato" beach bar having something to eat I got chatting to a bloke called Tony, who was originally from Liverpool, but was over in The Gambia to try and buy some diamonds.

Tony was a streetwise, hard looking man, of about 40 years old, who said that his boss was flying in the next day, and bringing a diamond tester with him, and if I wanted to I could borrow it to see if the diamonds I was being offered were genuine. I arranged to go over and see him the following day, and headed back down to the beach to track down "Fisherman", and get some samples from him. I found "Fisherman", got a small parcel of diamonds off him, and tucked them away, ready to meet with Tony the next day.

The following morning I drove up to "Leybato" beach bar where Tony was renting a small hut, and I went inside to meet his crew. Inside was like a scene from a bad "B" movie gangster flick. Tony was there with his "boss", who was also from Liverpool, and had a real ruthless air about him. He was heavily pockmarked, dripping in gold jewellery, and sipping from a tumbler full of whiskey as I entered the room. Completing the scene were a couple of Gambian "fixers", who were rolling joints, and laughing, and joking, with each other as I walked through the door.

I felt like I was from a different world to these characters, and I just wanted to test my diamonds, and get out of there as quickly as possible. The tester showed that the samples I had been given did register on the diamond scale, and as soon as I possibly could, I made my excuses, and left them to it.

"Fisherman" continued his grooming process over the next couple of months, always saying that there would be no money required from me up-front, and I continued to go along with it in the hope that I would be able to make a quick trip back to London, and return many thousands of pounds better off. We eventually got to the point where I said that I was ready to fly to London, and I asked him to furnish me with some diamonds for the trip. Suddenly the conversation began to take the direction of him wanting some money before he would give me the diamonds. I was adamant that this wasn't going to happen, and my "Fisherman" friend started to get menacing. It was hard to take him seriously because his face looked so soft, but James assured

151

me that he was a genuinely bad man, and I began to feel a bit uneasy.

Things finally came to a head one day on the beach. "Fisherman" had made up his mind that he wasn't going to take no for an answer, and I was equally determined that he wouldn't get so much as a penny from me up front. We had a bit of a Mexican stand-off on the sand, with him towering over me, and me being prepared to deal with anything he might do.

I felt so strong on the beach that there was no way I was going to back down. I really felt that I had home advantage, and out of the two of us he was the one who was out of his element. We faced off with each other for about five minutes, with him making an increasing number of threats, while I stared him down, and then he turned on his heel and left.

When he walked off I took stock of the situation. The whole diamond smuggling thing had been a brief foray into an alien world for me, and I had come away from it no better off, but without any drastic consequences either. It seemed to be par for the course for my life in The Gambia, so I quickly pushed it to the back of my mind, and soon forgot all about "Fisherman".

It was rainy season again, and I had a new adversary to threaten my daily happiness. The Portuguese Man o War jellyfish was a regular visitor to Gambian shores during the rainy season, and my daily swims soon began to involve a lot of manoeuvring to avoid being stung by one of these creatures. Fortunately they were only small examples of the species, but being stung was a painful and annoying experience.

The first sensation upon being stung was a burning pain in the area of contact, that increased in strength by the minute. At first when I got stung, I would immediately head back to shore, and dash into Kunte-Kinte to get some vinegar to pour on the sting, but after a while I just gritted my teeth, swore at the top of my voice, and carried on swimming. During these swims I would often get stung a number of times, and by the time I got back to shore, my arms, legs, and body, would be covered in red welts where the jellyfish had struck .

The Portuguese man o war also had a sting in the tail. Once the pain had worn off, the area afflicted would begin to itch terribly, and hundreds of little bumps would come up like mosquito bites. This itching would often keep me up all night, long after the pain had subsided, and I would curse my little transparent foes, as Adama slept soundly beside me.

It was obvious when the jellyfish were in town, because the beach would be strewn with dead ones that had been washed up on shore during the night. Most people avoided swimming when the jellyfish were around, but I was determined that nothing was going to stop me going for my daily swim, and I soon learned to accept jellyfish stings as part of normal life during the rainy season.

Another thing I would do at this time of year would be to make regular visits to Kartong, to stay at the Boboi Beach Motel. This was a magical place at this time of year. The trees in the compound were full of little yellow weaver birds, and the deserted beaches were my own private desert paradise. I would go for long walks along the deserted sands, and I found some very interesting things on my travels. Once I came across an enormous stingray that had been washed up on the beach. This leviathan was at least 2 metres wide, and was truly a sight to behold. I would find dead dolphins washed up on the shore, and there would be crowds of vultures pecking at the carcasses as I walked past.

153

At night thousands of crabs would make their way to, and from, the sea, and I would sit at the door of my tent smoking a roll-up, and watching them scurry about. Quite often the only other person I would see on my excursions along the beach was a wild looking man, dressed in a loin cloth, who would be carrying either a fishing rod, or a gun.

I asked David at Boboi Beach about this man, and he told me that he lived in the bush, and survived by catching his own food, either in the sea, or by shooting one of the wild pigs that roamed around the forest. There was something really attractive about this old man's existence, and I felt a real kindred spirit with him. I suspected that just like me he found that the hardest part of life was dealing with people, and he had made the decision to cut himself off from normal life, and live off the land.

I befriended him, and although we couldn't talk to each other, we developed a non- verbal method of communication that served us quite adequately. Occasionally he would give me a fish, which I would take back to the boys at the camp, and they would proceed to cook it for our lunch. Sometimes I would take a soft drink down to him, and we would sit with each other for a little while, just letting time pass, and enjoying each- others presence, without either of us feeling the need to try and start a conversation.

When I returned to the boat I told the boys about this man, and it turned out that he was Farmara's father. Farmara was deeply ashamed of his dad, and I wished that I could get him to see what I had seen. In Farmara's eyes his dad was nothing but a tramp, but I had seen a noble, and resourceful, man who was living life on his own terms.

I suppose that it's a common thing to want our parents to be what we want them to be, and more often than not they don't live up to our unrealistic expectations of them. I resolved not to mention Farmara's dad again specifically, unless he himself brought up the subject, but occasionally I would say something in his earshot that I hoped might help him to understand the choices his father had made, a little more than he seemed to at the time.

One day I decided to have a day off from the boat, and instead of going down to join the boys in the morning, I had a lie in, and then headed to The Leybato beach bar for lunch. I got there at about 1pm, and ordered a plate of Domoda, and a bottle of Malta. The restaurant was about half full, and I had a table to myself. As usual, the food was delicious, and the peanut stew was a great way to start the day. At the end of my meal I got up to take my plate back to the kitchen, to save the waiter a trip, and as I handed it to him, I noticed a commotion on the beach below.

A large group of people were standing by the water's edge, and they were shouting, and pointing out to the sea. I made my way down to join them, and when I got there I could just about make out a man floating face down in the sea, about 100 metres out from the shore. It was a Spring tide, and this was the most dangerous part of the beach by far. Large waves were crashing in every few seconds, and the current was sweeping everything towards the rocks that bordered this part of the shoreline. The man's friends were beside themselves with panic, but because the sea was so rough, everybody was too afraid to go in the water and attempt a rescue.

Without really thinking about it I immediately stripped down to my shorts, and plunged into the water. The sea was lovely and warm, but the waves were large, frequent, and very powerful. Luckily I had been training myself for the last two years in this particular stretch of the Atlantic Ocean, and after a bit of a struggle I managed to get out beyond the surf. As I struck out

155

toward the man, who was lying face down in the water, I could see that he was not making any signs of movement.

At the same time that I had gone into the sea, a Gambian lad had plunged in as well, and we reached the man almost simultaneously. Luckily for us he was almost finished, and had long since lost consciousness. He was a big man, possibly 17 or 18 stone, and if he had been struggling for his life he could have taken me, the Gambian lad, or possibly both of us, down with him.

When a man is drowning the vice-like grip he will often exert on his would-be rescuers can easily be fatal for all concerned. Fortunately for myself , and the Gambian lad this man had no fight left in him, so we grabbed an arm each, turned him over onto his back, and slowly began dragging him back towards the shore. After battling the waves for what seemed like an eternity, we finally pulled him up onto the beach, and then we slumped down exhausted on to the sand. Somebody immediately began to try and resuscitate him, and after one final push on his chest, he began to splutter, and cough. An ambulance was called, and he was carried off, placed in it, and taken to Banjul hospital.

I had no idea if he was going to make it or not, but there was nothing else that I could do. In the water, he had seemed pretty much dead, and I knew that he had been unconscious for quite a while. His lungs had undoubtedly been filled with water, and it was possible that he had suffered brain damage as a result of oxygen starvation. I consoled myself with the fact that I had done everything I could, and then walked down the beach to join my friends, and colleagues, down at the boat.

I was living so much in the now that I didn't give the man much of another thought for the rest of the afternoon. It wasn't callousness on my part, it was more that the incident had just seemed like part of daily life over here, and I didn't expect a big fanfare, or any recognition, for what to me had seemed the natural thing to do under the circumstances.

Also, daily life in this part of the world had hardened me to any tragedy, and whether the man had died or not seemed no worse to me than the deaths of the hundreds of small children every rainy season from malaria. The fact that the man was white, and British, may have meant more to his friends, but it didn't to me anymore.

When we packed up on the beach for the day, I decided to go for a steak at one of the English bars that were dotted around the area. They were showing an English football game on the T.V, and I munched my dinner quite happily, while watching Manchester United play in the Champions League. After the match finished, I walked outside to the area at the front of the bar, where there were a number of tables with people eating. As I walked towards the exit, a loud round of applause broke out from one of the tables. People were looking at me, and clapping, and cheering. I didn't know what to do so I gave a little bow, and walked over to them.

It turned out that they were the friends of the man that I had helped to pull out of the sea that afternoon, and they told me that although he was shaken, and shocked, there seemed to have been no lasting physical damage. They couldn't thank me enough for saving his life, and I must admit that it felt pretty good to be the hero of the hour. I thought of the Gambian lad who had also been part of the rescue, and I wished that he had been around to get some of the plaudits.

At the time of the incident things had happened so quickly that there had been no time for any kind of thanks, and I suspected that all his efforts had probably gone unrecognised. It had been a good opportunity for the Gambian lad to shine, and I felt a little guilty that I had stolen some of his thunder.

Anything that happened in that part of the world was an opportunity for someone, and I hoped that the Gambian lad had been financially rewarded for his efforts. I asked the man's friends if they had thanked him, and they said that they had given him a few hundred Dalasis. That made me feel slightly better, as at least he hadn't gone away empty-handed from his act of unselfish bravery.

Chapter 13 – Betrayal

A couple of weeks later, when I went to the beach, there was a nasty surprise waiting for me. James told me that a Dutch friend of his had bought him a boat, and that he was going to put it right next to mine on the beach. I was furious, but I did my best to not show it. I had given James a fantastic deal as the skipper of my boat, and now it felt like he was totally betraying my generosity by putting himself in direct competition with me.

I didn't mind that he was striking out on his own, God knows if I had been in his shoes, and someone had offered to buy me a boat, I would have bitten his hand off, but I did mind that he was going to set it right next to mine, on the same part of the beach, and then was acting like it was no big deal.

Things went from bad to worse pretty quickly. The following morning James's boat arrived on the beach. It was a far superior boat to mine. It was bigger, better equipped, and really looked the business. My heart sank as I looked at it. I was proud of my little boat, and the niche that I had carved out for myself on this part of the beach, and James's actions had ruined my peace of mind. Inwardly I was seething, but I told him what a great boat it was, and wished him luck.

With the benefit of hindsight I wish I had told him exactly what I thought of him. He probably wouldn't have taken any notice, but it would have been a more honest way of dealing with the situation, and the resentment that was starting to build up in me would have been slightly alleviated.

Solomon stepped up to the plate and offered to be my new skipper so I readily accepted, and unbelievably put him on the same self- sabotaging deal that I had given to James. Every day after that when I went down to the beach, I would feel annoyed when I saw James's boat, and the idyllic little life that I had created began to feel stressful and irritating. A saying in one of the support groups I went to was that "resentment is the number 1 offender", and I had let my resentment with James go unchecked, and untreated, and consequently I began to slowly unravel.

Things came to a head one day when I was returning on the boat, from a fishing trip, with Solomon at the helm. We were approaching the shore, and Solomon was trying to get his timing right, so we could ride in on the surf, and I suddenly felt freezing cold, and terrified. It was about 95 degrees Fahrenheit, and the waves weren't any bigger than usual, but I was convinced that Solomon was going to capsize the boat, and I didn't want to be on it when he did.

I told Solomon that I'd see him on shore, and I dived off the side of the boat, and into the crashing waves. I somehow made it back to the beach, and when I got there I realised that all of my confidence had evaporated. The role that I'd been playing as a Gambian fisherman for the past three years had taken its toll on me, and I realised with horror that I had nothing left to give.

In the UK I had been dependant on prescription medication, pretty much from my early twenties up until I went to The Gambia, so I sought out a local Gambian doctor, and obtained a supply of anti-depressants, Valium and anti-psychotic medication. I began to take the Valium before I went to the beach in the morning, to try and recreate the feelings of euphoria that I used to have before James's treacherous act, and my spectacular loss of confidence. It didn't make any difference to the way I was feeling, and I quickly worsened. I started to have days when I wouldn't go to the beach at all, and instead would stay in bed all day, and take

160

handfuls of antipsychotics to get me through the long uncomfortable hours.

These days would be tortuous. It would get to about 3pm, and the heat would be unbearable, the drugs would just exacerbate the feelings of panic, and I would lie there sweating, and trying to hold it together, paralysed by the anti- psychotics, and the tremendous feelings of dread that threatened to overwhelm me.

One day after taking an overdose of antipsychotics, I collapsed in the doorway when Margaret was talking to me. Poor Margaret must have wondered what on earth was going on, and soon after this incident she said she was leaving. I begged her to stay, because without Margaret the house would cease to operate. Margaret did pretty much everything in the house, from looking after Joe, to doing the shopping, cooking the evening meal, and cleaning, and tidying the house. Also she was a breath of fresh air, and it was her cheerfulness that made the house into a home.

To my total relief she said that she would stay, but I was unable to change my behaviour, and I gradually got worse, and worse. Everyone became more and more concerned about me, and Adama couldn't understand what was happening to her once-capable husband. Eventually things got so bad that Adama said that we should go and see a medicine woman in her mum's village. I was so desperate by now that I was willing to try anything that could possibly make me feel better, so we took a bush taxi to Sifoe to see her.

We got there in the early afternoon and went to a small mud hut where the woman lived. We were ushered in by her assistant and led to where the woman herself was seated. She spoke no English but began muttering away to herself in a tribal dialect. She touched my forehead, and the chanting got louder, and louder, until eventually, with a final flourish, she produced a small worm, from a pot that she had by her feet.

I asked Adama what had happened, and she told me that the medicine woman said that she had pulled the sickness out of my body, and the worm represented the evil spirit that had invaded me.

We gave the woman a few hundred Dalasis, left Sifoe, and returned to Mangi. Unsurprisingly I didn't feel any different after my visit to the medicine woman, and I carried on with my tortuous self-medicating routine, with no regard for anyone else around me. I didn't realise it at the time, but I had triggered my previous addiction to prescribed medication, and now it was a juggernaut that threatened to overwhelm my family, myself, and everything around us.

The dream had turned into a nightmare. My self-medicating was getting worse every day, and I knew that if I carried on in the same vein I wouldn't last much longer. I had applied for a British passport for my son a few months previously, and I got a call from the British embassy to tell me that it was ready to be picked up. Also, ever since I had been in The Gambia, I had been gathering information, and accumulating proof of the validity of my marriage to Adama, so that when the time came to apply for her U.K visa we would be totally prepared. I had pictures of our wedding day, pictures of us together on consecutive New Year's Eve's dinners at the Senegambia hotel, and somehow or other I had made sure that we met all the financial requirements for a successful application.

The time had come for me to leave The Gambia, and I knew that I couldn't leave without my family. It was far from certain that Adama's application would be successful, and the next few weeks were a tense time as I tried to collate all the necessary information and put together a credible application for her. Finally, we were ready, and we submitted Adama's application to live with me, in the UK, in January 2006.

Roughly a month after submitting the application, Adama was given a date for an interview. We were both very nervous, and in the evenings we rehearsed questions that she might be asked. It was a deadly serious time for us both. I knew that I couldn't return to the UK without Adama, and Joe, and I knew that if I stayed in The Gambia much longer the levels of self-medication that I was taking would probably kill me sooner, rather than later.

It might sound daft that I couldn't just stop this self- destructive behaviour, but by now I was in full-blown addiction to prescribed medication, and without some kind of professional input, I was on a rapidly accelerating downward trajectory.

The one good thing that we had in our favour was Adama. As I have said, she was exceptionally clever, and she applied herself to our interview rehearsals diligently. When the time came for her to present herself at the embassy, I said a heartfelt prayer to the higher power that I believed had kept me sober for all the years since I had last taken a drink, and I prayed that our little family would somehow be able to stay together.

I dropped Adama at the embassy gates and headed on down to the beach. When I got home that night Adama was already there, and I grilled her about her interview. She seemed to think that it had gone pretty well, and now all we could do was wait until she was called back for a decision, which she had been told would probably be within the next few weeks.

I coped with the ensuing week's thanks to my friends on the beach. They all knew how ill I had become, and they knew that this visa was a matter of life or death for me. Abu had looked me in the eye one day and said very firmly that if I stayed in The Gambia I would die. He didn't need to tell me, I knew. I also knew that returning to the UK wouldn't solve my recently triggered addiction problems but concentrating on getting the visa was what was keeping me going, so I focussed on that, and tried to keep the feeling of impending doom at bay as best as I could.

Chapter 14 – Back for Good?

When Adama got the call a few weeks later, my heart was in my mouth. She took a taxi to the embassy this time, because the car was with Omar in the garage, and I sat at home with my head in my hands, trying not to take too many tablets. She walked back in the door two hours later, and as I looked at her face, my heart sank. She looked grim, and crestfallen, and not happy, and joyful, as I had hoped. "Mr Coughlin", she said, "we are going to England."

It had been another masterful tease by the expert mickey taker. She had got the visa, and now there was nothing to stop us all getting on a plane back to my little flat in King's Cross. By this time I had completely run out of money, so once again I turned to my dad for help. He sent me the money for our tickets back to the UK, and we set about preparing ourselves for leaving The Gambia as soon as we possibly could.

The last two weeks I spent in The Gambia were all about saying goodbye. My friends on the beach were genuinely delighted for myself, and my family, and they wished us all the best for our new life in Great Britain, with Solomon adding again that I had found myself a "good sister" in Adama. I left the boat, and all the gear, with Solomon, with the idea that one of Adama's relatives would come to the beach from time to time to collect my share of the takings. I knew that this was unlikely to work, but it was the best I could do at the time.

I said goodbye to my ex-pat friends that I had met along the way, and as I went to, and from, the beach, I said goodbye mentally to all the dusty streets, the little children playing football, and the stray dogs, and cats, that made up the landscape of Manji. I said

165

goodbye one final time to the beautiful Atlantic Ocean that had been my haven, and my training ground, for the past three years, and I said goodbye to my boat "Mac's Spirit", that I hoped would be around for years to come, to keep alive the name of my mother, in this little part of West Africa. The hardest goodbyes were to Adama's family, especially to Margaret, who had been a shining light in our little compound, and without whose help Adama and I would not have managed nearly as well as we had.

When all the goodbyes were said, and done, we took a taxi early one morning to Banjul airport to get our flight back to England. I had no confidence at all that I was doing the right thing, but keeping the family together seemed to be the most important thing to do, and although I felt terrible in myself, I consoled myself that at least I had been successful in doing that.

On March 22nd 2006 we stepped on board the aeroplane that was to take us back to the U.K. Little did I know, as the plane took off, that in barely a year I would have lost my family, be living on the streets, and just about to start my first prison sentence.

The years that I had spent living in The Gambia had taught me a lot about myself, and a lot about a different way of life, but it hadn't solved the problem of my alcoholism, and when I came back to England that particularly rapacious creditor was ready, and waiting, for me, and about to take me on a horrific rollercoaster ride that was to nearly cost me my life.

The End

Adama and Joe are now living in Manchester. Adama works in healthcare, and Joe is studying for his "A" levels.

My dad is now 87 years old, and still lives on his own in Nottingham

My brother and I haven't spoken for over 17 years.

Margaret and "baby" Val are both alive and well and still live in The Gambia

Adama's mum is alive and well, and still lives on the family compound in Sifoe.

David, Rory, and Caroline still live at the Boboi Beach Motel in Kartong. Maryama passed away from breast cancer.

I lost contact with Julie, and was never able to discover if the book about Minh-To was ever completed.

Minh-To popped up in "The Daily Mail" a couple of years ago, and appeared to be alive and well and living in the Manchester area.

I never saw, or heard from Maurice, and Anna again, but they remain as friends in my memories.

I never saw or heard from Hortensia again.

My good friend Maison died from an overdose shortly after I returned from The Gambia.

Acknowledgements

7 years after returning from The Gambia, and after an horrific period in my life, I was finally able to write this book. It has taken me 4 years to complete, and after numerous edits, and re-writes, I am finally satisfied that it is a true representation of the time I spent in The Gambia.

I would like to thank my dad for financing the entire adventure, my friend Povl for helping with the editing process, and my friends, Lewis, and Rebecca, for entertaining me in their house, and helping me with the final stages of getting it to print, which I would never have been able to do without them.

Finally, a massive thank you to the people of The Gambia, for adopting me as one of their own, and showing me that it really is "Nice to be nice"

15% of any royalties received from the sale of this book will be donated to a Gambian children's charity.

About the Author

Rob Coughlin was born in 1964 to Anglo-Scottish parents, and grew up near Park Royal, in North West London, in the 1960's and 70's.

His various jobs and careers have included being a trainee site agent, a despatch rider, a betting shop manager, a tax collector, an HGV driver, a labourer for a stonemason and a tree surgeon, and running his own small fishing business in The Gambia for 3 years.

He has a 17 year old son who lives with his mother in Manchester, and he now lives by the sea, in North Somerset, with his long haired, Maine Coon, cat Roche.

His first book "Toubab" was published in 2019 and documents the 3 years he spent in The Gambia living and working as a local fisherman.

He is currently working as a delivery driver to support his writing.

Printed in Great Britain
by Amazon